Ripley's —"Believe It or Not!"

6th Series

Ripley's busy research staff has gathered these strange facts, wondrous sights, and apparent miracles to entertain and amaze you. Find out about the extraordinary world you live in and the unusual marvels it contains!

If you cannot find your favorite **Believe It or Not!** POCKET BOOK at your local newsstand, please write to the nearest Ripley's "Believe It or Not!" museum:

175 Jefferson Street, San Francisco, California 94133

1500 North Wells Street, Chicago, Illinois 60610

19 San Marco Avenue, St. Augustine, Florida 32084

The Parkway, Gatlinburg, Tennessee 37738

145 East Elkhorn Avenue, Estes Park, Colorado 80517

4960 Clifton Hill, Niagara Falls, Canada

Central Promenade, Blackpool, Lancashire, England

Ripley's —"Believe It or Not!"

6th Series
is an original POCKET BOOK edition.

Ripley's Believe It or Not! titles

Published by POCKET BOOKS

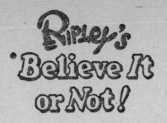

6th Series

PUBLISHED BY POCKET BOOKS NEW YORK

RIPLEY'S BELIEVE IT OR NOT!® 6th SERIES

POCKET BOOK edition published September, 1958

3rd printing......................October, 1975

This POCKET BOOK contains material from *Ripley's 35th Anniversary Believe It or Not!*, published March, 1954, and *Ripley's Mammoth Believe It or Not!*, published March, 1955.

L

This original POCKET BOOK edition is printed from brand-new plates made from newly set, clear, easy-to-read type. POCKET BOOK editions are published by POCKET BOOKS, a division of Simon & Schuster, Inc., 630 Fifth Avenue, New York, N.Y. 10020. Trademarks registered in the United States and other countries.

CONTENTS

Contents

Ripley's
°Believe It
or Not!

Imperial Gratitude

WHEN PRINCE ABDERRAHMAN BEN HIQUEM (1778–1859) was ten years old, there were 31 claimants to the throne of Morocco ahead of him. One day his horse shied under him and precipitated the young Prince into the Moghreb River, turned by rain into a raging torrent. None of his suite dared plunge after him as the strong current carried the boy to his doom. Suddenly, a 20-year-old shepherd named Ali ben Muhammad appeared on the scene, leaped into the roaring river without a moment's hesitation and pulled the boy to safety.

Thirty-five years later a series of multiple deaths in the imperial family cleared the way to the throne, and Abderrahman became Emperor of Morocco. The shepherd, now 55 years old, heard the news and rejoiced. For many a weary month he walked from his mountain village to the capital of Morocco, hoping to claim his long overdue reward.

When he reached the imperial palace in Marrakesh, he

was promptly admitted to the Presence. With tears streaming down his face he knelt down and, embracing the royal feet, announced that he had come "to collect his reward for saving the august life of His Majesty" thirty-five years before.

Abderrahman sat a long while plunged in deep meditation. At last he spoke, and his voice was hardly audible. "By the Beard of the Prophet, your reward shall not be withheld."

As Ali looked up expectantly, the Emperor turned to his executioner who was standing by with a bared broadsword in his hand: "I order you to take this man outside and to chop his head off. I have spoken."

"But I saved your life," said the shepherd in a voice choked with terror. "Do I deserve death for saving you from drowning?"

"No. I may appear to you cruel and ungrateful. But remember that I am your emperor. No amount of gold—however large—would ever be considered adequate payment for what you have done. And lest it be said that the saviour of my life went unrewarded, I regret you must die."

*   *   *

MURDER

THE MURDER BRAND
—
6 MEN LOST THEIR LIVES IN A QUARREL OVER THIS STEER.
— SO THIS BRAND WAS PUT ON HIM!
Brewster County
Texas.

THE EVER SITTING MAN

The Eternal Sitter

YUEN TONG, a Chinese Buddhist ascetic of the eighteenth century, sat down at the age of twenty-two and never arose from his sitting position for sixty-two years. The attitude is ritually known as Dhyana Mudra or Meditation and is one of those fantastic endurance ordeals which leave a Westerner gasping with astonishment. He died without arising and at his direction his mummified body—frozen in the identical squat he had so long endured in life—was enshrined in a glass case within the Pagoda of the Rocks in Yun-nan-fu, China, in 1760.

*　　*　　*

THE BACKBONE of a camel is perfectly straight.

A Book Written in Blood

THE JAPANESE EMPEROR SUTOKU (1124-1164) wrote a book
in his own blood. While he was an exile in Sanuki for three
years, he spent the entire time copying the Lankavara Sutra
(a famous Hindu religious essay) using his own blood as
ink. This unique work consists of 135 pages, 1215 lines,
10,500 words and was written in the pious hope that Buddha
would reward him by a restoration to the throne of Japan.
Sutoku was reinstated in 1144 and ruled for another twenty
years.

THE GIRLS WHO MARRY FLOWERS

The Bride of a Flower

GIRLS OF THE KADAVA KANBI caste in Baroda, India, have reason to envy all of their sisters in the whole wide world. They have the poorest chance of finding a husband. There is only one day in which they may marry and that lucky day comes only once every twelve years. Since a ten-year-old girl is considered an old maid, their status is deplorable indeed. If there are too many girls in one family and they do not wish to chance waiting twelve years, they may resort to a curious technicality. They may contract a legal marriage to a bouquet of flowers. As soon as the blooms fade, the girl is considered a widow. In this particular caste the widow's lot is vastly brighter. A widow is not restricted to one day out of every 4,380 but may grab a husband any time, while her unmarried sisters are powerless to compete with her.

THE ENGLISH WALNUT is not English. It is Persian.

*   *   *

THE MARRIAGE ceremony of the Manbhao in the Amraoti district of India consists of a man transferring his purse or wallet to the object of his affections. If she accepts it, they are man and wife.

*   *   *

THE AMERICAN ROBIN is not a robin. It is a thrush.

*   *   *

A WINK is equal in duration to 3/10 of a second.

*   *   *

THE FUNNY BONE is not a bone. It is a nerve.

*   *   *

A CHICKEN grows more than 8,000 feathers.

*   *   *

IF YOU HAVE a rosemary bush in your garden, you have a living memorial of Queen Philippa of Hainaut (1314-1369), consort of King Edward III of England. It was she who introduced the flower into England from her native Belgium in the 14th century. Rosemary from her English garden was transplanted to all parts of the British Empire and to what is now the United States of America.

*   *   *

SOUR HONEY is produced by stingless bees in the state of Goyaz, Brazil.

*   *   *

$$1^2 = 1$$
$$11^2 = 121$$
$$111^2 = 12321$$
$$1111^2 = 1234321$$
$$11111^2 = 123454321$$
$$111111^2 = 12345654321$$
$$1111111^2 = 1234567654321$$

THE DIAMOND in the flag of the State of Arkansas indicates that the state has the only diamond mine in the United States.

* * *

THE JEWISH New Year can never fall on either a Friday, Sunday, or Wednesday.

* * *

PROMETHIUM, a by-product of atomic fission, costs 1½ billion dollars an ounce.

* * *

"SARDONIC" is derived from a plant, Ranunculus Sceleratus, also known as the Sardinian Herb. It grows in Sardinia, was formerly used in medicine and was so sour that it convulsed the faces of all who partook of it. Because it twisted the features into the semblance of a bitter, mocking laugh, such a face-twisting smile became known as Sardinian or Sardonic.

* * *

MEN who marry sisters but are otherwise unrelated to one another are considered brothers-in-law in the United States but nowhere else on earth.

* * *

EBRIATE and Inebriate mean exactly the same thing.

* * *

CHEMICAL TOWNS in the U.S.A.:

Soda   Lithium
Carbon   Radium
Calcium   Vanadium
Cobalt   Ozone
Gold   Potash

* * *

MAINE is the only state pronounced as one syllable.

THE STRANGE PYRAMID DANCE OF THE POROJAS

A TWO-STORIED DANCE is an obligatory marriage rite performed by invited guests at weddings of the Poroja tribe in the State of Bastar, Central India. The dance is an all-night affair performed by 12 men. Six of them climb upon the shoulders of the other six and after linking arms dance round and round, both those on the ground and those higher up. Then the high dancers climb down and serve in turn as the base of the pyramid. The longer they dance, the greater is their friendship for the principals. There is a tribal belief that the young couple is assured of 10 years of happy married life for every hour the pyramid dance has lasted.

*   *   *

THE PRICE of salt was its weight in gold in Oregon in 1852.

The 41-Year Fast

THE GRAND RABBI JUDAH MEHLER (1660-1751) fasted 6 days of every week for 41 years. He was 50 years old when he embarked upon a life of such austerity as to have no equal in history. He fasted from Saturday night to the following Friday evening each week, completely abstaining from food and drink. He only broke his weekly fast on the eve of Sabbath, eating and drinking sparingly for a period of 24 hours. He also broke his fast a dozen times a year in deference to the Jewish holidays. In spite of this rigorous regime, he led a busy life as the rabbi of the three communities of Cologne, Cleve and Deutz, Germany. He attended to his pastoral duties most conscientiously and lived to the respectable age of 91.

9

CHARLES DELAHAYE
famed French tennis star
ONCE PLAYED 4 SETS IN THE FULL UNIFORM OF THE
FRENCH NATIONAL GUARD – *CARRYING FIELD PACK AND
MUSKET WITH FIXED BAYONET!*
DELAHAYE WON THE MATCH 3-1 ALTHOUGH HIS OPPONENT WAS
CONVENTIONALLY DRESSED

*　　　　*　　　　*

THE PRAYING MANTIS is worshipped as a divinity by the
Bushmen of South Africa.

*　　　　*　　　　*

A GOLD NUGGET in the shape of a man with a pack on his
back. Found by A. W. Stewart, Petaluma, Calif.

*　　　　*　　　　*

COUNT NESSELRODE (1780–1862), after whom the Nesselrode Pie was named, was Foreign Minister of Russia for
forty years, yet he never learned to speak Russian.

*　　　　*　　　　*

WILLIAM TELL is the son-in-law of Rip Van Winkle. Alham-
bra, Calif.

A Commander-in-Chief in Diapers

THE YOUNGEST commanding general to "lead" an army into battle was the three-months-old Duke Godevaart (Godfrey) III of Brabant (Belgium). He was only 90 days old when he succeeded his father as sovereign of Brabant and leader of its army. As soon as the infant was on the throne, war broke out, and it became the baby's duty to "lead" his army into battle. He was placed in a cradle in charge of a nurse who strapped him between two trees on the battlefield. He was thus present in person, and the victory won on that day was credited to him. During his reign of 48 years (1142-1190), he was known as "The Courageous," although History has also commemorated him less flatteringly as "The Cradle Duke."

11

The Ravens of St. Benedict

FOR THE LAST 1400 years the Benedictine Monastery of Subiaco, Italy, first of the twelve monastic establishments founded by St. Benedict, has kept one or more pet ravens, descendants of a crow that saved the founder's life in the sixth century. The bird had snatched a poisoned slice of bread from St. Benedict's hand, just in time to save him from death. The tame bird was henceforth kept as a pet and its progeny in an unbroken line has been befriended by this ancient monastery ever since.

*　　　*　　　*

YOU are 65% oxygen.

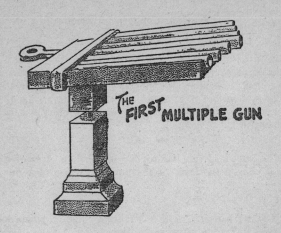

The Prototype of the Ack-Ack Gun

THE FORERUNNER of a modern multiple anti-aircraft weapon was dredged up from the bottom of the Pacific Ocean where it lay submerged for 38 years. It was found off the New Hebrides in 1826 in the wreckage of the French vessel *La Boussole,* which had gone to the bottom without a trace in 1788. The seven-barrelled gun, an astounding anticipation of a modern weapon, could fire seven projectiles simultaneously, was mounted on a massive pedestal which could be depressed or raised to any point of aim.

* * *

MICROSCOPIC WILL

ENGRAVED BY A SAILOR ON AN IDENTIFICATION DISK WAS ADMITTED TO PROBATE.

The Roundabout Marksmen

THE NATIVES of Ecuador hunt the large Arrau turtle of the Amazon basin with bow and arrow. The arrow is not aimed at the turtle as it could never penetrate the tough carapace of the animal. The hunter discharges the missile high in the air where it describes a parabola before it lands on the turtle's shell from a great height. It is this high trajectory that is fatal to the turtle.

* * *

IF A HANDFUL of salt be dropped into half a glass of water, will it change the level of the liquid? (See answer on page 150.)

* * *

HOW MANY half-dollars does it take to equal 15 silver dollars (in weight)? (See answer on page 150.)

* * *

IF 10 SHEEP jump over a fence in 10 minutes, how many jump over in an hour? (See answer on page 150.)

* * *

WHAT WORD contains five double letters in succession? (See answer on page 150.)

* * *

THAAAAI, a 7-letter word containing 6 syllables, is a Kikuyu greeting, meaning "Long Life and Health."

* * *

RED BUTTER is highly prized by the Chilas of the Hindu Kush. It is butter which has been stored for a hundred years.

* * *

YAK'S milk is pink.

* * *

21978 is quadrupled when inverted (87912).

TURKEY GOBBLER
HATCHED ITS MATE'S EGGS
Owned by
MRS. C. W. McGEHEE
Jackson, Miss.

THE MOST AMAZING MARKSMEN IN THE WORLD

A STICK
OF **RED** SEALING WAX
FLASHED BEFORE THE EYES
ALWAYS APPEARS **BLACK**

THE JOCKEY CAP
Prince Island, Portuguese Guinea
NATURAL ROCK FORMATION

ASK, ME.
IS A
TOWN
IN THE
U.S.A.

A BLACK EYE is called a Blue Eye in Germany and a Poached Eye in France.

*   *   *

IF STRESSED on the second syllable, anathema means "cursed." If on the third syllable, it means "divine."

*   *   *

A BRUSH used to apply varnish gives 100 times as much wear as one used to apply paint.

*   *   *

JOHN MOTTLEY, English dramatist, was the author of *Joe Miller's Joke Book*. Joe Miller, a dour actor, could not read or write and never uttered a joke in his life.

*   *   *

THE WINDOWS in an empty house will never frost—no matter how low the temperature.

*   *   *

COVERED WAGONS ORIGINATED THE *TRAFFIC SYSTEM* OF *PASSING TO THE RIGHT!* IN AMERICA

The Oldest Business Sign in Existence

It is 2500 years old, was found in Memphis, Egypt, and is now in the Cairo Museum. It reads: I RHINO OF CRETE INTERPRET DREAMS BY GOD'S COMMAND. Advertising fraternity, please note that the first commodity on record ever advertised in public was DREAMS.

*   *   *

A needle and thread has been given to every student of Queen's College, Oxford, England, every New Year's Day since the College was founded in 1340. This is to remind the students that the founder's name was Eglesfield, expressed as "Aiguille Fil"—French for "needle (and) thread."

*   *   *

Calanus, a Greek sage and legislator who was a lifelong sufferer from colic, passed a law banishing every kind of stomach ache from the Greek Empire (4th century b.c.)

MIAN MADAN

A Crown for a Clown

MIAN MADAN, a strolling performer of India, played his way
to a throne.

In 1416 the inhabitants of the State of Suket (350 square
miles, population 60,000) in the Punjab, India, removed their
rajah for incompetence. To find his successor they resorted to
the most startling talent hunt in history. All the leading stage
stars of India were invited to take part in a great historical
drama—to be enacted in the garden of the Royal Palace of
Suket. The entire adult population of the state was to witness
the performance. The actor receiving the greatest volume of
applause was to be acclaimed Rajah of Suket.

The winner was a wandering comedian named Mian Madan.
The acclaim he received was so deafening that all his fellow
players conceded his victory in advance. He was taken directly
from the stage and seated on the *gadi* (throne) of Suket. He
reigned for twenty-six years under the traditional name of
Madan Sain and his descendants ruled the state till India became a sovereign democratic republic in 1949.

A Church Waited 620 Years to Be Built

WHEN KING LOUIS IX (St. Louis) landed in Carthage, Africa, in 1270 on the Last Crusade, he vowed that he would erect a great cathedral on the beachhead if Carthage became French. Shortly thereafter the king died of the plague and the Crusade was abandoned. But the king's vow was not forgotten. It was kept alive for more than six centuries. In 1881 Carthage, now known as Tunisia, became a French Protectorate. The French Cardinal Lavigerie determined to act at once. He directed a world-wide appeal for funds—but limited his solicitation to the descendants of the Crusaders. In spite of the long lapse of time a sufficient number of crusading scions were found to realize St. Louis's pledge. With their contributions the first stone was laid in 1884 and the glorious structure first envisioned by the saintly French king was completed and dedicated on May 15, 1890.

19

BEES IN THEIR BONNETS!

THE CHAPEAU OF A WELL-DRESSED GIRL OF THE FOULAH TRIBE IS A PORTABLE BEE HIVE!

Fouta Djallon, Fr. West Africa

*　　　*　　　*

IF YOU WALK 100 miles east, 100 miles south, 100 miles west and 100 miles north, you will not arrive at your starting point. Why? (See answer on page 150.)

*　　　*　　　*

THE LEOPARD cannot change its spots. It has none. The so-called "spots" are in reality rosettes—terminologically entirely different.

*　　　*　　　*

THE STARS and Stripes—hallowed by usage—are neither stars nor stripes. The correct heraldic term is "mullets and barrulets."

20

Athletic Motherhood

MOTHERS in the mountainous regions of Piemonte, Italy, carry their babies, cradles and all upon their heads. They often cover great distances thus encumbered—including journeys of many hours—without showing any sign of fatigue.

* * *

THE BIBLICAL Prophet Daniel was nominated as the FIRST PRESIDENT. ("It pleased Darius to set over the kingdom . . . three presidents: of whom Daniel was FIRST." Daniel 6:1–2)

* * *

THE THIRD hand on a watch is the SECOND hand.

* * *

A SQUAD of eight soldiers marching in single file—in a different order each day—will require 110 years before they will return to the original order.

The Conquering Calendar

CAPTAIN ALBERT PAULIS of the Belgian Army conquered a kingdom at the point of an almanac. He also saved his own life and that of twenty subordinates.

On February 18, 1905, Captain Paulis and twenty of his men were captured by Sultan Yembio of Mangbetu and Azande, Africa. The sultan had the well-earned reputation of a cannibal.

Paulis's life and that of his subordinates hung by a thread. On the morning of his fatal interview with the sultan, the captain idly glancing through an almanac, learned that the day was to be marked by a partial lunar eclipse beginning at 8 P.M. A thought flashed through his mind. He remembered having read in his boyhood of just such an opportunity that saved the lives of Columbus and his crew during their Fourth Voyage to the New World in 1503. He decided to act at once.

Summoning to his tent Basongonda, youngest son of Sultan Yembio, he opened the palaver by stating: "Go tell your father that if he dares to harm me or any of my men, I have the power to destroy him with a wave of my hand. Tonight when the moon will be about there [here he indicated a spot in the sky], I shall raise my hand and cause the heavenly luminary to die. The death of the moon will foreshadow the death of your father, the sultan. But if you change your mind, I can still stay the death of the orb of night in the last minute."

That evening both the sultan and his son came to test the power of the white man's magic. At 8 P.M. Paulis raised his hand and flicked it in the direction of the silvery disk. Immediately father and son launched a cry of terror when they beheld a black shadow biting into the edge of the queen of night. They prostrated themselves and buried their foreheads in the dust. Out of the corner of their eyes they watched in fascination as darkness continued to devour the silvery disk. They lamented and entreated their captive to avert the disaster to the heavenly body in the last minute. Paulis seemed to relent. "It is still in my power to revive the

THE KINGDOM CONQUERED BY AN ALMANAC!

moon," he said, "and I'll do so but on one condition. We must immediately undergo the rite of 'bakole' [exchange of blood] and you must recognize the authority of the King of Belgium over yourself and your country." "We promise" —exclaimed the sultan and his son. "You are a great sorcerer. Yembio wants to be your brother and the son of your king." They prostrated themselves again and poured sand over their heads and chests in sign of submission. Then they watched Paulis raise his hand again. Uttering a few cabalistic words he waved the devouring shadow away from the half-

23

darkened moon. There was an explosion of joy when the two royal savages saw the shadow beginning to recede.

Their country became a part of the Belgian Congo. With its area of 82,000 square miles and a population of 770,000, it is still a part of that Belgian possession.

Lovey Dovey

THE MOST PECULIAR Pigeon Fancier in all history was Khanderao, the immensely wealthy Gaikwar of Baroda, India, who ruled his fabulous state for fourteen years (1856–1870). His special extravagance was staging weddings for his pigeons with all the Oriental ostentation and love of display. He spent 100,000 rupees ($48,500) three times each year so that a pair of selected doves from his cotes could be married according to the laws of the state with all the princely magnificence of the royal house. The feathered bride and groom rode to their nuptials on a state elephant covered with gold brocade and dripping with jewels. The Gaikwar himself officiated at the ceremony and then gave a royal feast which all the notables and officials of his domain were bidden to attend. Costly gifts to the newlyweds were compulsory. The Indian Croesus spent a total of 2 million dollars on forty-two pigeon weddings for the sake of indulging his peculiar hobby.

Silver Spoon Babies

THANKS TO John Wagstaffe, a poet of Bawburgh, Norfolk, England, at least one child of poor parents is born with a silver spoon in its mouth each year. Wagstaffe, who died in 1809, left 50 pounds to be invested in gilt-edged securities. He directed that the income be used to purchase one silver spoon each year—said spoon to be placed in the oral cavity of the first child of the year born of poor parents in Bawburgh. The fund has been faithfully administered since 1809.

THE WEDDINGS OF THE LOVE BIRDS

*   *   *

THE SHEEP of Larzac, France, whose milk yields Roquefort cheese, never drink water. The region is arid but the pastures are lush. The shepherds do not allow their flock to find water—for fear that it would coarsen both wool and flesh. The animals obtain all their needed moisture from the rich grass.

25

SPIDER PAGODA - PEIPING

A Spider Pagoda

CHI CHU T'A (the Chinese equivalent of our caption) in Peiping was built over the mortal remains of a common variety of garden spider. The Buddhist priest Yu An was engaged one day in the reading of the Diamond Sutra, one of Buddha's sermons. Suddenly he was diverted by the sight of a spider—rapidly climbing up the legs of his reading table. It sat down on the table top, bowed its head and seemed to listen to the recital of the sacred lesson. The action was repeated several times till the preacher and the arachnid became friends. When the spider died it was promptly "identified" as the reincarnation of one of the Boddhisatvas, future saviors of the world. The identification was so strong that its tomb was honored by the erection of a tall, elaborate and richly carved pagoda which is still standing.

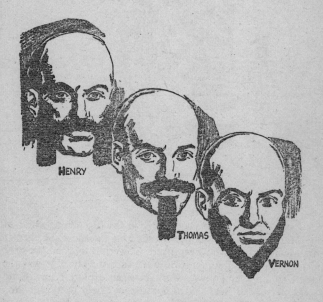

HENRY

THOMAS

VERNON

THE THIBAULT TRIPLETS
of New York
THEY WERE SO IDENTICAL
THAT THEY GREW
WHISKER INITIALS
1895

The White Indian Chief of the Mandan Tribe was 7 FEET TALL and WHITE AS SNOW

The Giant Albino

SHAKAKA (1758–1812), better known as Big White, chief of
the Mandan tribe of South Dakota, was the most spectacular
American Indian who ever lived. Towering to a height of 7
feet—his hair and complexion were snowy white. He was the
tallest albino ever known. The American explorers Lewis and
Clark persuaded Shakaka to accompany them to Washington
in the winter of 1806–7. His arrival in the nation's capital
was a long-remembered sensation. Washington Society, headed
by President Jefferson himself, turned out to make Big White
the lion of the season. He returned to South Dakota and was
killed by an enemy Indian on November 28, 1812, while up-
holding the cause of the United States against Great Britain.

PADRE KINO Italian Jesuit

CARRIED THE WORD OF GOD TO THE SOUTHWEST - 1687 - 1711
FOUNDED 20 CITIES - BAPTIZED 40,000 INDIANS AND
WAS THE FIRST TO DISCOVER CALIFORNIA WAS NOT AN ISLAND

HE NEVER TOOK SALT IN HIS FOOD - BUT ADDED BITTER HERBS INSTEAD
NEVER DRANK WINE OR ENJOYED A SIESTA - NEVER UNDRESSED FOR BED -
SLEPT BUT ONE HOUR A NIGHT WITH HIS SADDLE FOR A PILLOW

29

RÉTIF
de la
BRETONNE

The Most Original Author in History

NICOLAS-EDME RÉTIF DE LA BRETONNE (1734–1806), French printer and novelist, was the author of 203 books of which 152 WERE NEVER WRITTEN. The author simply transferred their contents from his brain directly to the printing press. It was said of him that he could literally think in cold type. The literary merit of most of his books is unquestionable although some of them have been described as licentious. They were widely read in the eighteenth and nineteenth centuries and enjoyed many editions.

* * *

SOME DIAMONDS are harder than others. The hardest diamond known to history is a 5¾-carat gem owned by a diamond cutter in Kimberley, South Africa. The stone has defied all attempts to cut it and still weighs the original 5¾ carats, in spite of three years' treatment on the diamond cutter's wheel. It even turned the tables and bit into the cutting plate. The owner has given up all hope of ever taming the obdurate jewel, and retains it as an expensive curiosity.

MR. AND MRS.
LORD
LIVE MIDWAY BETWEEN
2 CHURCHES
in
Georgetown, Texas

EVERY
MEMBER of the CHOLA-AYMARA TRIBE, Peru
HAS WORN THE SAME STYLE HAT
FOR 421 YEARS!

IT IS PATTERNED AFTER A HELMET
PRESENTED TO A YOUTH OF THE TRIBE
BY FRANCISCO PIZARRO IN 1531

THE
MOST MAGNIFICENT
MILESTONES IN HISTORY
ELABORATE TOWERS **25** FEET HIGH
WERE BUILT BY EMPEROR AKBAR THE
GREAT OF INDIA *TO MARK EVERY MILE
OF ROADS IN HIS EMPIRE!*

"THE BASKET CASE" GENIUS

RODRIGO RAMIREZ DE SAAVEDRA Y VINENT, Marquis de Villalobar (1866–1926), was one of the most remarkable men who ever lived. He was a full colonel in the Spanish Army, and in succession Spanish Envoy to Lisbon, Washington, and Brussels. He was a member of the Royal Academies of Madrid and Brussels, commander of the Arsenal in Zaragoza (Spain), honorary citizen of the four Belgian cities of Brussels, Ghent, Liége and Antwerp, doctor of the universities of Liége and Bruges. All this despite the fact that he was born practically "a basket case"—without legs and with only one arm. He was the Spanish Envoy in German-occupied Belgium during World War I and became famous as the fearless defender of Edith Cavell, the English nurse whom the Germans executed in 1915.

NATIVES of the Kimpoko Tribe, Africa WEAR THEIR HAIR IN A PERFECT IMITATION OF A SAILOR'S CAP —COMPLETE WITH RIBBONS

THE INDESTRUCTIBLE LEAF FORMED BY A DROP OF MOLTEN STEEL Submitted by THOMAS JOHNSON, Donora, Pa.

THAT'S "GROUNDS" FOR A SUIT

COFFEY AND POTT DROVE 2 CARS THAT COLLIDED in Santa Barbara, Calif.

O'ROURKE'S FORD — County Sligo, Eire IS NEVER CROSSED BY ANY MAN NAMED O'ROURKE AN ANCIENT CURSE AGAINST A PAGAN PRINCE NAMED O'ROURKE IS NEVER DEFIED

*   *   *

How Long is a Moment?
(See answer on page 150.)

*   *   *

A WITNESS in an Indian court of law is considered more credible if he has gold in his teeth. Lying is a serious offense for a man whose teeth are plugged with gold.

The Rule of Three

THE CHURCH OF THE TRINITY in Waldsassen, Bavaria, has 3 towers and 3 turrets—each of which has 3 lucarnes and 3 dormer windows. It has 3 small and 3 large crosses, 3 roofs, 3 vents in each roof, 3 windows and 3 doors in each section of the edifice, 3 sections in each tower and turret. Inside there are 3 altars with 3 finials, 3 staircases, 3 doorways, 3 lights, 3 transept arches, 3 columns, 3 niches, 3 windows in 3 bays, and 3 statues of the Virgin. The builder was Georg Dientzhofer, third architect of his family. The completion of the structure required 33 months, 33 weeks, and 33 days—and cost 33,333 florins and 33 kreuzer.

*   *   *

A SNAKE in the London Zoo was fitted with a glass eye.

The Strangest Phobia of a Genius

PROFESSOR PHILIP ANTON EDUARD LENARD (1862–1947), an experimental physicist who belonged to the greatest figures of his time, suffered from a morbid horror of the name of Sir Isaac Newton. He could not bear to pronounce it himself—see it written—or hear it spoken. Whenever it became necessary to use the name in the course of his lectures, he would turn his back on the classroom, allow someone to write it on a blackboard, to be expunged before he could resume his lecture. This phobia—one of the most mystifying in history—afflicted a man who was professor of experimental physics at the universities of Heidelberg and Kiel, who received a Nobel Prize for Physics in 1905 and who was a shining light in the field of electrons, cathode rays, fluorescence and phosphorescence, "a dark genius beclouded by a pathological fear of one innocent combination of letters and sounds."

PROF. LENARD

BUILT BY A POEM Tus, IRAN

The Most Poetic Bridge in the World

THE BRIDGE OF TUS (Iran), which crosses the Keshef-rud (river), was literally built by a poem. The epic was the "Shahnama," consisting of 60,000 verses, penned by Firdausi (932–1020), the most celebrated of all Iranian verse smiths—the Homer of Iran. Firdausi's patron was Sultan Mahmud el Ghazni (998–1030), who instructed the state treasurer to pay the poet a gold piece for each verse. When the masterpiece was completed thirty-five years later (1011), an elephant load of silver was substituted for the promised gold. The poet reacted in characteristic fashion. He divided the 60,000 pieces of silver into three parts. One-third was given as a tip to the elephant boy. One-third paid for a single bath and the remaining one-third—equal to about 2 million dollars today—was used to pay for a single glass of beer—the most highly paid refreshment in history.

Later the sultan had a change of heart and rectified his error. He sent a camel caravan laden with gold to Tus. But it was too late. The gold-bearing train passed a funeral array on the road. It was the mortuary procession of the great poet. When his widow received the Sultan's ransom, she turned it over to the city authorities to pay for the construction of a bridge over the Keshef-rud. The city of Tus has long vanished, but the Bridge Built by a Poem is still standing and is still in daily use after nearly a thousand years.

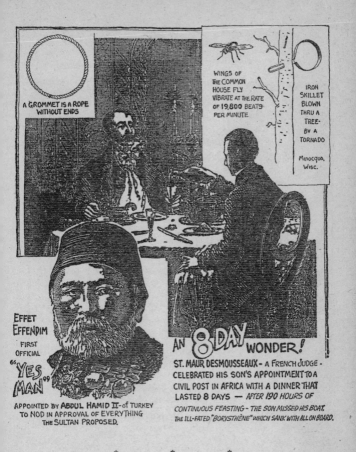

A GROMMET IS A ROPE WITHOUT ENDS

WINGS OF THE COMMON HOUSE FLY VIBRATE AT THE RATE OF 19,800 BEATS PER MINUTE

IRON SKILLET BLOWN THRU A TREE— BY A TORNADO

Minocqua, Wisc.

EFFET EFFENDIM

FIRST OFFICIAL

"YES MAN"

APPOINTED BY ABDUL HAMID II—OF TURKEY TO NOD IN APPROVAL OF EVERYTHING THE SULTAN PROPOSED.

AN 8 DAY WONDER!

ST. MAUR DESMOUSSEAUX – A FRENCH JUDGE – CELEBRATED HIS SON'S APPOINTMENT TO A CIVIL POST IN AFRICA WITH A DINNER THAT LASTED 8 DAYS — AFTER 190 HOURS OF CONTINUOUS FEASTING – THE SON MISSED HIS BOAT. THE ILL-FATED "BORYSTHÈNE" WHICH SANK WITH ALL ON BOARD.

*   *   *

IF THE ENDS of a 10-foot rope are drawn 2 feet closer together, how many feet would the rope sag? (See answer on page 150.)

*   *   *

PRESIDENT James A. Garfield could write Latin with one hand and Greek with the other—simultaneously.

THE HERO WHO WAS FRIGHTENED TO DEATH BY A SALT SHAKER

FIELD MARSHAL NICOLAS-AUGUSTE DE MONTREVEL
(1646–1716)
French veteran of a hundred battles

WAS SO SUPERSTITIOUS THAT HE
WAS FATALLY STRICKEN

WHEN A DINNER GUEST SPILLED THE SALT

*   *   *

A CLOCK weighs more after it has been wound. As it runs down, its weight decreases.

*   *   *

BIANNUAL means "occurring twice a year."
BIMONTHLY means "occurring once every two months."

STRANGE ACT OF A GOD-TREE

DURING A STORM – A GIGANTIC GOD-TREE FELL ACROSS
A ROAD FORMING A NATURAL ARCHWAY.
San Martin Zapotitlan, Guatemala.

* * *

WHAT TWO natives of Kentucky were Presidents of the United States at the same time? (See answer on page 150.)

* * *

THERE IS more iron in steel than there is in cast iron.

* * *

A BUSHEL of wet wheat weighs less than a bushel of dry wheat. Wheat swells when wet and fewer grains will be required to fill the bushel.

* * *

A SPRIG OF lilac sent to one's betrothed in medieval England was an indication that the engagement was broken.

* * *

THE CANADIAN RIVER rises in New Mexico, flows through Texas and Oklahoma to Arkansas, but does not come near Canada.

SIR
ISAAC
HOLDEN
(1807-1897)
British Wool Merchant

ATE THE SAME FOOD
TWICE EACH DAY FOR 48 YEARS!

The Most Enduring Appetite

SIR ISAAC HOLDEN (1807-1897), millionaire wool manufacturer of England, ate the same breakfast and supper every day for the last 48 years of his life. His breakfast and supper, always identical, invariably consisted of a baked apple, a banana biscuit, an orange and 20 grapes. He attributed to his unvarying diet his lifelong perfect health and freedom from any ailment till he died at the age of 91.

* * *

ST. JOHN'S WORT, a poisonous weed, is only harmful to white-haired cattle and sheep. Even where the animal only has a small patch of white, it will die from eating the weed. All other animals are immune to the poison.

Life's Steps

OKHMAN, a poor foundling of Lahore, Pakistan, lived for 62 years upon the marble steps of the Mosque of Vazir Khan in Lahore. He was abandoned there by his parents at the age of 5, and from then on the white marble steps were the only home he knew. Supported by the charity of pious visitors, he lived, ate and slept there in every kind of weather, never leaving his perch until he died at the age of 67 (1913).

* * *

KING ADOLF FREDRIK (1710–1771) of Sweden had seven sweethearts in a row. Two were one-eyed, two were one-legged, two were one-armed. The seventh had no arms at all. His opinion of love would be a shock to our romantic notions. He claimed that true love was based on pity.

The Church Built by a Mendicant

THE MAGNIFICENT Church of Our Lady of Miracles in Saronno, Italy, is a miracle in itself. It was built by a beggar. He was a helpless invalid named Pedretto who was cured by prayer in 1460. After his recovery, he determined to translate his gratitude into a House of God. The fact that he was penniless did not deter him. For 38 years he stood on the highway begging alms from passersby and travelers. He never used a penny of the proceeds for himself. In 1498 he had sufficient money to begin the construction of the sumptuous church but never lived to see it finished and dedicated 83 years later.

* * *

THE SMALLEST unit of time in Tanjore, India, is the kainodi, literally "the snap of a finger." 60 snaps constitute one naligai (24 minutes).

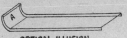

OPTICAL ILLUSION

GAZE AT "A" AND THE SLED
APPEARS TO TILT
Drawn by
FRANK LEFFELL
Baltimore, Md.

The **KING** of Abeokuta, Africa
WAS CHOSEN TO RULE
500,000 NATIVES
BECAUSE HE HAD WORKED
AS A BANK TELLER!

*THE ELECTORS REASONED
THAT HE WOULD BE AN EXPERT
FINANCIER*

The CITY THAT FLOATS ON THE SEA
A MIRAGE METROPOLIS

COMPLETE WITH HOUSES - STREETS - PARKS
AND GARDENS OUTLINED IN PINK - WHITE
AND GREEN APPEARS SPORADICALLY ON
THE SURFACE OF THE MEDITERRANEAN
NEAR MAZARA DEL VALLO, SICILY

A *SPRIG* OF THE
SERPICULA VERTICILLATA PLANT
WILL PURIFY
A PAIL OF STAGNANT WATER

STRANGEST PLANT IN THE WORLD

THE WELWITSCHIA - Southwest Africa
ONE FOOT TALL - 15 FEET IN CIRCUMFERENCE - PRODUCES
ONLY 3 LEAVES WHICH LAST THRU THE LIFETIME OF THE PLANT —
WHICH IS ABOUT 100 YRS.

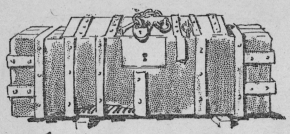

THE MARRIAGE CHEST

MEDIEVAL ENGLISH churches were usually equipped with a heavy parish chest which was used as a pre-marital aptitude test by prospective young brides. To pass this test, a candidate for marriage had to lift the 30-pound lid with one hand. If she flunked, she was considered too weak to cope with the tasks of a housewife, and the groom could call the whole thing off.

Queen for a Day

HISTORY KNOWS only one queen whose reign did not exceed 24 hours. She was Juana de Castro, who married King Pedro I of Castile in May 1354. The marriage took place at Cuellar, Spain, and two bishops officiated at the royal nuptials. No one knows what happened. The next morning the King had the marriage annulled and left without ever seeing her again—although he lived 15 years longer.

* * *

PANDOLFO NABONNA of Lucca, Italy, named his five children ETRAPANOUB, PANOUBETRA, NOUBETRAPA, BENOUPATRA, and OUBETRAPAN—each name an anagram of Buonaparte.

* * *

A RACE HORSE named "Seventeen Sixty" won and paid $17.60. Amarillo Tri-State Fair, September 20, 1934.

THE
LONGEST
NAME IN
HISTORY

The Name Prodigy

RAJADHIRAJ RANAJI SHRIPRUTHU SINGJI (1732), ruler of the
State of Mahi Kantha, in the Gujarat division of Bombay,
India, used what is to all purposes the longest name in history.
Although the original version contained only thirty-two letters,
he lengthened it enormously by insisting that every reference
to him must repeat his full name 108 times—no more no less.
Orally and in writing, in books and on monuments the name
could not be mentioned except by expanding it to 108 times its
original length. Whenever the master affixed his name to a
document, a secretary always stood by to repeat the signature
107 additional times. This had the effect of inflating the name
to 3,456 letters—sufficient to fill about two pages of solid
print in the "Believe It or Not" book. State historians and
courtiers deemed this whim the dominating bane of their
existence.

An Island of Solid Salt

THE ISLAND of Ormuz, in the Persian Gulf, is a solid cylinder of kitchen salt rising from the ocean bottom to a height of 300 feet. This gigantic inhabited salt plug measures about 16 miles in circumference and was thrust up by a prehistoric upheaval from the floor of the Gulf. Nothing can grow on the hard sterile soil, and all water is strongly saline.

*   *   *

THE LEGAL standard measure in the United States is neither the yard, foot nor inch but the meter of 39.37 inches.

*   *   *

SIMONIDES OF CEOS (556-467 B.C.), one of the most illustrious poets of ancient Greece, was the first author who demanded and received pay for writing. He was the first to have made a business of literature—the first to have made it pay and therefore the first modern author. He was publicly crowned as poet laureate for 53 years in succession.

The Imperial Compass

THE EARLIEST compass was used in China more than 1700 years ago. It was a little steel man standing on a revolving base made of magnetic scales, so constructed that the man always pointed south. It was used as a figurehead and guide on the carriage of the Chinese emperor in the year 235 A.D.

What Is This Fellow Saying?

THE 800-MILE-LONG Aruwimi River in the Belgian Congo was named by David Livingstone who was the first white man to see it. He inquired of a native, "What is the name of this river?" The answer was "Aruwimi," meaning "What is this fellow saying?" Livingstone misunderstood and named the river Aruwimi. The forest through which it flows, covering an area of 25,000 square miles, has been named the Aruwimi Forest.

THE MAN WHO REFUSED MILLIONS
JOZSEF HADIK-BARKOCZY

The New Woman

JOZSEF HADIK-BARKOCZY of Hungary at the age of fifty-one (1892) filed an action in the Hungarian courts to have himself legally adjudged a woman. He was neither a transvestite nor one of the borderline cases with which newspaper readers have become familiar in the last few years. Hadik-Barkoczy was the last direct heir to a million-dollar fortune which he had no desire to accept. Under the old Hungarian feudal law it was impossible for a male to refuse such a succession. But Jozsef was so determined not to become a millionaire that he resorted to the legal fiction of joining the opposite sex in the eyes of law. The courts agreed and the succession passed to a lateral line. The New Woman never changed his mode of life. The only concession he made to his new status was that he altered his Christian name from Jozsef to Jozsefna (Josephine), prefacing it with a "Mrs." instead of "Mr."

* * *

ENAMEL of the teeth is the only body tissue that cannot repair itself.

THE "FLOATING" STONE of TAY MINH, ANNAM

A Nightmare of Wood and Stone

ONE OF THE most fearsome sights on earth is the little Temple of Tay Minh in the kingdom of Annam—one of the Associated States of Indo-china. The structure lies directly beneath a gigantic boulder—weighing every bit of 300 tons. The stone seems to be suspended in mid air, an inch above the roof of the frail edifice. There is nothing to hold the crag in place—except a complete reversal of the laws of gravity. For those hardy souls who wander fearlessly in and out of the sanctuary there is the ever-present danger that any instant might be their last. It is hard to describe the feeling of dread that overwhelms one at the prospect. A frozen nightmare, a spine-chilling optical illusion, a diabolic camera trick are some of the impressions that cause a perfectly sane man to doubt his own senses.

*　　　*　　　*

THERE are 47 different kinds of headache.

49

A tied horse is FAST.
A running horse is FAST.
Colors that do not run are FAST.
A playboy is FAST.
If you do not eat you FAST.

*　　　*　　　*

THE TURTLE has not changed in 200 million years.

*　　　*　　　*

pir	vent	venir
un	vient	d'un

This French syllabic arrangement reads: *Un soupir vient souvent d'un souvenir.* (A sigh often comes from a memory.)

*　　　*　　　*

THE RUSSIANS may have exploded a thermo-nuclear bomb, but they will never be able to boast of an H-bomb. They have no letter H in their alphabet.

*　　　*　　　*

A RAISIN dropped into a glass of champagne will continue to rise and fall in the glass.

*　　　*　　　*

A WOMAN breathes 1/3 faster than a man.

*　　　*　　　*

Here lie I
Killed by a Sky
Rocket
In my Eye
Socket
　　　　—Penryn Churchyard, England

*　　　*　　　*

O.K.　　　　　　Yo Yo
No Go　　　　　Inky Poo
Turn Turn　　　Keep It
are localities in Queensland, Australia.

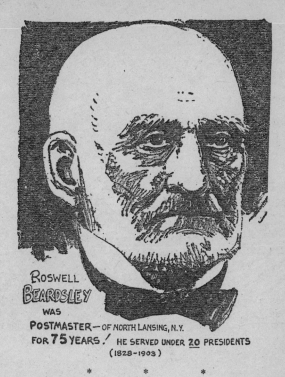

ROSWELL **BEARDSLEY** WAS **POSTMASTER** — OF NORTH LANSING, N.Y. FOR **75** YEARS! HE SERVED UNDER **20** PRESIDENTS (1828-1903)

*   *   *

How FAR does the house move? The rollers are one foot in circumference and the house is moved one complete revolution of the rollers. (See answer on page 150.)

The MOVING HOUSE

The Bayonet Was Stronger Than the Blizzard

ONE OF THE strangest battles in history arrayed an army against a snowstorm and the army won.

In January 1797 two French divisions under Generals Bernadotte and Delmas rushed to Napoleon's aid from the Rhine to Italy. They crossed the Swiss Alps in the dead of winter—which was memorable for severity that year. A sudden tempest of great violence stopped them in their tracks. Even the hardboiled Alpine guides quit, saying it was useless to go on. The whirling snow obliterated all mountain paths

and reduced visibility to zero. Fatigue and the great cold
became irresistible. Demoralized soldiers began to lie down
in the snow to face death by freezing. Suddenly a shrill
sound, carrying above the fury of the gale, rent the air.
The trumpeters of the commanding generals blew the signal
for the charge. Weariness and despair vanished in an instant.
They fixed bayonets, beat their drums and with flags whip-
ping in the storm attacked the most elusive enemy of all—
the weather. For once, man was victorious over the ele-
ments. They conquered in the most uneven hand-to-hand encounter and crashed through to Italy—before the Austrians
knew that they had left their positions on the Rhine.

SALISBURY CATHEDRAL, the most beautiful in all England—"a great chiseled diamond in a setting of emeralds," has been endowed by its builders with a rich profusion of calendar features. It has as many doors as there are months in the year —as many windows as there are days—as many pillars as there are hours—as many sculptures as there are minutes in an hour—as many consecration crosses as there are seconds in a minute. The striking number of pillars has been noted in a rhyme:

As many marble pillars here appear
As there are hours throughout the fleeting year.

The spire of the cathedral leans 22½ inches out of the perpendicular.

THOMAS HANDFORD, of New Mills, Lancashire, England, held the local jail in such affection that he bought it and converted it into his residence. He was a reformed drunkard and poacher who served many a term in the town clink. After ten years of total abstention from drink and petty crime he saved enough to purchase his former prison and live in it the remainder of his life—all by himself. This happened in 1854. The former hoosegow is still owned by the Handford family.

*   *   *

BENJAMIN CONSTANT (1767–1830), celebrated French writer and politician, wrote a book of five volumes—comprising 2,500 pages—using as a manuscript the backs of playing cards.

REV
FATHER
GABRIEL RICHARD
OF DETROIT, Michigan
THE ONLY CATHOLIC PRIEST
EVER ELECTED TO CONGRESS

THE LUCKY PUNCH!
DANNY LONDON
BORN DEAF AND DUMB WAS HIT IN THE HEAD IN THE BOXING RING *AND SUDDENLY FOUND HE COULD BOTH SPEAK AND HEAR!*
Brooklyn, N.Y. 1929

THE "BOGEYMAN" BEECH
Burnham, England
NATURAL TREE FORMATION

MACHINE
FOR COMPOSING HEXAMETER LATIN VERSES
BUILT IN SOMERSETSHIRE, ENGLAND · 1843
IT CONTAINED 86 WHEELS, CYLINDERS, CRANKS, SPRINGS, PULLIES ETC. WHICH ARRANGED LETTERS TO FORM VERSES

WEAPONS FOR A COLD WAR!—
2 CANNON CARVED FOR EMPRESS ANNA IVANOVNA OF RUSSIA **FROM BLOCKS OF ICE!**
THEY WERE ACTUALLY FIRED IN 1740 WITH BALLS OF ICE AS AMMUNITION

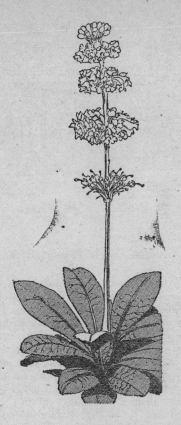

The Bloom of Doom

THE ROYAL COWSLIP (Primula Imperialis) grows only on one spot on earth, on the solitary peak of the 10,000-foot-high volcano, Pangerange, in Java. The natives call it the Bloom of Doom. Whenever it appears, it is a sure indication of an imminent volcanic eruption. The Javanese search for it with foreboding and prepare to flee as soon as they see it.

THE TOWEL

The Oldest Towel Service

A FRESH TOWEL has been furnished daily since 1541 to ornament the casket of Gazi Husrev Beg who is entombed within the Great Mosque of Sarajevo, Yugoslavia. Gazi, who was also the founder of the mosque, made a curious provision in his will. He directed that 500 ducats be invested with the Administration of the Sanctuary. The income was to defray the cost of a clean towel—changed daily—that was to be draped upon the sarcophagus. Visitors to the mosque who come to view the grave wash their hands in symbolic innocence and dry them on the clean towel.

The long-range towel supply service has been uninterrupted since 1541. Many wars, famines, sieges and disasters have ravaged the city in the interim—World War I started here. But they have been unable to stay the towel delivery which is still going on at the present time.

*　　　*　　　*

IF A PAINTER uses a brush TWICE as big will he get through TWICE as quickly or half as fast?

(See answer on page 150.)

The Tree of Obedience

The costliest tree in the world today—costliest in human effort and sacrifice—grows in Wadi 'n Natrun, a barren section in the wilderness known as the Thebaid Desert in Egypt. It took more than 1,600 years to cultivate it to its present size, and its tremendous cost in labor and devotion is beyond computation.

In the year 346 a saintly hermit named Abba Amoy took a dry stick of almond wood and planted it in the thirsty desert sand. He told his disciple, a young man named John the Short: "Water this stick from your own water jar till it shall bear fruit." The task was a superhuman one. The nearest well was so far away that it took all night to fetch water for the tree and to bring it back. The messenger had to forego his nightly rest with no hope for making up for lost sleep in the daytime. But such is the power of obedience inspired by religious devotion that John continued as a water carrier, sacrificing sleep, for three years. Then the stick began to bear almonds. John took the kernels and offered them to a neighboring monastery with the words: "Take and eat the fruits of the Tree of Obedience." The sacrifice has been continued for more than sixteen centuries, enabling the tree to bloom in the middle of the most forbidding desert in the world—with not a blade of grass within a hundred miles. All during this time a successor of John the Short has stood ready to water the almond tree by sacrificing his sleep. Altogether it has taken half a million man-days of labor. Multiply 500,000 days by the amount of a man's daily wage, add to it half a million nights of relinquished rest and it becomes clear why this is called the costliest tree in existence.

*　　　*　　　*

Water Streams Capable of Drilling Through a Pine Plank

WHEN HIGH-CARBON steel is heated and cross-rolled, tough scale forms on the surface. To remove the disfigurement, the glowing steel is blasted with streams of water of such terrific pressure and force that they could drill right through a heavy pine plank.

*　　　*　　　*

THE SEA CUCUMBER explodes and blows out its internal organs when it runs away from an enemy. If it escapes, it grows new internal organs.

Elizabeth
BILLINGTON

THE MOST preposterous charge ever made against an artist was leveled against Elizabeth Billington (1768–1818), the greatest singer England ever produced. She had a voice of such sweetness, compass and power that after she sang in Naples, Italy, on May 30, 1794, in "Inez di Castro," an opera expressly written for her, she created such a furor that the Neapolitans accused her of having caused the terrible eruption of the Vesuvius volcano which occurred on June 15, 1794. The general excitement reached such a pitch that she escaped being lynched only by precipitate flight. No other singer in history has ever been singled out for so dangerous a compliment.

Miss Billington was steeped in a musical background. Her father was a famous oboist, her mother a celebrated singer; her brother was a noted violinist; her husband played the double bass and her brother-in-law was a high-powered harpsichord player.

THE **SCULPTURED ROCKS**
ROTHENEUF – FRANCE
HUNDREDS OF QUAINT AND STARTLING FIGURES
HAVE BEEN CARVED OUT OF THE SOLID ROCK
BY ABBÉ FOURÉ – A HERMIT WHO SPENT
THE LAST 20 YEARS OF HIS LIFE CONVERTING
A STONE DESERT INTO THIS WEIRD ART GALLERY

"BLACKIE"
A WOODCHUCK
THAT LIKES
ICE CREAM
CONES
–
Crawford
Notch
State
Park,
N.H.

THE **MOST** AMAZING LEXICOGRAPHER
IN HISTORY!
JOHN COLERIDGE PATTESON
1827–1871
Bishop of Melanesia
COMPILED **25** DICTIONARIES
*EACH IN A LANGUAGE
HE HAD JUST LEARNED!*

THE **DASSIE** OF AFRICA· SMALLER THAN A RABBIT –
IS THE NEAREST LIVING RELATIVE OF THE ELEPHANT!

The Lowly Pretzel Is a Blueblood

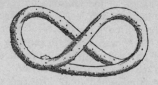

THE PRETZEL was invented by no less a celebrity than Charlemagne (742–814), King of the Franks and first Emperor of the Holy Roman Empire. When he subdued the heathen Saxons more than eleven centuries ago, he forced them to bake the sign of a cross into all their bread and pastries in token of their conversion to Christianity. It was in compliance with this order that the pretzel was born. It received its name in Italy from its resemblance to a pair of crossed human arms *(brachiatelli)*. Longer than any other product of the baker's trade, the pretzel resisted the inroads of the machine age. Down to our own time it had to be twisted by hand. But lately even the pretzel had to yield its privileged status. A fantastic new machine now fashions pretzels with all the skill of an expert pretzel bender—at greater speed. Tireless steel fingers loop and tie the dough into a perfect product of the pretzel maker's art with a complete absence of vibration.

The Strangest Coat of Arms

THE OFFICIAL BADGE of the German university city of Tübingen. is an old judicial murder. It dates back to the year in which Columbus discovered the New World.

In 1492 a poor wandering baker boy was arrested in Tübingen and charged with the murder of his road companion. Although the prisoner tearfully pleaded his innocence, he was condemned to death. The sentence was executed by breaking the condemned man's body on a wheel. Shortly thereafter the baker's supposed victim appeared alive and whole on the scene. He was aghast at the miscarriage of justice and reported it to the German Emperor Maximilian I. The latter castigated the city and ordered it to be branded henceforth with a coat of arms depicting the judicial murder. The Broken Baker has been the heraldic emblem of the city ever since.

Felix ZIEM
Noted French Painter
WAS HIS OWN HEIR!

His Own Heir

FELIX ZIEM (1821–1911), a gifted French painter of Croatian origin, lived for many years aboard a bark in a Venetian lagoon—where a tentlike structure on deck served as his studio.

After he won fame and fortune with his sun-and-light-drenched Venetian landscapes, he withdrew to an old house in the Rue Lepic in Paris, where he lived like a hermit. In 1908 the eighty-seven-year-old artist was falsely declared dead. His fortune was about to pass into the hands of relatives—while the testator was still very much alive. Ziem applied to the authorities to revoke his death certificate and to restore him formally to the ranks of the living. But he was told that such a procedure would take too long. In order to thwart his relatives in a hurry he was advised to execute a will in his own favor. Such a testament was duly drawn and promptly filed. Through its probation Ziem became his own heir and testamentary beneficiary, to enjoy the fruit of his own labors for an additional three years.

The Most Extraordinary Village

PSYKHRÉ, in Crete, is inhabitable during only nine months of each year. In the spring, summer and fall it is a pleasant green settlement—sheltering and feeding sixty-four inhabitants. The approach of winter is a very serious matter. The villagers empty their houses of all contents and desert the hamlet for three months. After their departure millions of gallons of water rush in with a tremendous roar and convert the village into the bottom of a deep lake. Psykhré remains completely submerged for a quarter of a year. With the advent of spring the waters recede, the bottom of the erstwhile lake dries out, the inhabitants return and the settlement resumes its normal, cheerful appearance. The abnormality has its explanation. Psykhré is completely walled in by a mountain range. For nine months of the year the rivers, streams and torrents of the region escape through a cleft known as "Kathavotron" (The Swallow's Hole). The cold season seals the crevice with a sheet of ice. With its egress cut off, the waters rapidly transform the village into a raging sea. The inhabitants have long become accustomed to the fury of the season and bear with equanimity their very precarious existence.

*　　　*　　　*

The Rhyming Will

(Probated in London on July 17, 1789)

> I GIVE and bequeath
> When I'm laid underneath
> To my loving sisters most dear
> The whole of my store
> Were it twice as much more
> Which God's goodness has given me here.
> And that none may prevent
> This my will and intent
> Or occasion the least of law-racket
> With a solemn appeal
> I confirm, sign and seal
> This the true act and deed of
>
> Will Jacket.

THE **ENCHANTED MIRROR** INSCRIBED WITH THE NAMES OF THE 4 ARCHANGELS INCANTATIONS AND MAGIC SQUARES – IS BELIEVED TO MAKE EVERY GIRL LOOK BEAUTIFUL AND TO FULFILL HER HEART'S MOST SECRET DESIRE

THE **UNDER-WATER VILLAGE** – Psykhré, Crete. MOST EXTRAORDINARY VILLAGE IN THE WORLD PSYKHRÉ IS INHABITABLE ONLY DURING THE SPRING AND SUMMER! AS WINTER APPROACHES THE INHABITANTS ABANDON THEIR HOMES AND THE WATERS RUSH IN TO SUBMERGE THE VILLAGE COMPLETELY FOR THE WINTER

ALEXANDER **HAMILTON** STUDIED LAW ONLY 4 MONTHS TO BECOME ONE OF THE GREATEST LAWYERS IN THE UNITED STATES

Kaiserslautern.

THE COAT OF ARMS of the city of Kaiserslautern, Germany, is based on a tall fish tale involving a pike that lived 267 years (1230–1497) in the fishpond of Emperor Frederick II.

CAPTAIN AAGE CARLSON
Aalborg, Denmark
Remarried HIS WIFE 92 YRS. AFTER HE DIVORCED HER!

There Were Giants in Those Days

CAPTAIN Aage Carlson of Aalborg, Denmark, was cast in so heroic a mold that no other record is ever likely to equal it. It all began innocently enough when our hero took to himself a wife at the age of twenty in 1811. Matrimony had a strange effect on Aage. He was seized with an irresistible wanderlust. After a long conversation in which he tried in vain to induce his bride to share his nomadic life with him, he decided not to stand in the way of her happiness and divorced her. "I shall always love you," he said in a tone of

68

deep conviction. "But since you decline to roam the seven seas with me, it is only fair to give you a chance to find happiness with my successor." Aage left Denmark in 1811 and nothing further was heard from him during the remainder of the nineteenth century. With the dawn of the twentieth century rumors reached the ex-Mrs. Carlson that her former husband was still alive and that he was thinking of settling down in his native country. In 1903 Aage Carlson returned to Aalborg and called upon his ex-wife whom he had not seen in ninety-two years. Mrs. Carlson received him with dignity and reserve. When Aage learned that she had never remarried, he sank to his knees and delivered a proposal of remarriage couched in such ardent terms that her resistance melted away. They remarried in 1903 and lived long enough to celebrate the rarest of all matrimonial events —the hundredth anniversary of their original wedlock. Both died a year later.

LITTLE SURE SHOT

THE FIRST HOLIDAY GREETING CARD IN AMERICA WAS SENT OUT BY *ANNIE OAKLEY* — THE FAMOUS MARKS*WOMAN* OF THE WEST

HE 'DUDE' IT

PRINCE WENZEL VON KAUNITZ-RIETBURG

The Dandy of Dandies

PRINCE WENZEL VON KAUNITZ-RIETBURG (1711–1794), Austrian Chancellor, was the most clothes-conscious man who ever lived. For 57 years he changed his apparel completely 30 times a day. Since we must assume that he suspended such activity during his 8 hours of sleep, it would appear that he donned a new change of habiliments every 32 minutes of the 16 hours left. The action of dressing and undressing required 4 hours daily. Gentlemen of the Rococo period dressed with greater care and their vestments were both more numerous and more elaborate than the male garb of today. It included not only laces and decorations but also rings, snuff boxes, sashes, fobs, chains and as many as six watches with each suit. They also indulged in cosmetics, face patches and powdered wigs. Kaunitz spent $400,000 a year on his wardrobe alone and his passion for changing consumed an uninterrupted 10 years of his lifetime. With clothing activity at so high a pitch it is a wonder he found time for anything else. Yet this fop was the leading figure in European politics for 42 years—masterminding wars and political action and affecting the lives of hundreds of millions of people—with great vigor and acumen.

THE GREAT ROCK IN HOREB

To A MAN enamored of the Scriptures there is no more thrilling site than the Great Rock of Horeb, in the Sinai Peninsula between Egypt and the Holy Land. It is here that one of the great biblical miracles was enacted. Jehovah commanded to Moses: "Behold, I will stand before thee there upon the rock in Horeb; and thou shalt smite the rock, and there shall come water out of it, that the people may drink" (Exodus 17:6). "And Moses did so"—the Bible continues—"in the sight of the elders of Israel." The actual rock still stands upon the spot trod by Moses. Sweet water flows from it today as it has for the past thirty-five centuries. A "Believe It or Not" expedition drank deeply from it and found it just as refreshing in 1936 as the Israelites must have done in 1491 B.C.

THE GOLDEN NOSE

The Emperor with the Golden Nose

EMPEROR JUSTINIAN II of Byzance (669–711) lost his nose and replaced it with a nose of solid gold. He first ascended the Byzantine throne in 685 at the age of sixteen. After an unhappy reign of ten years he was overthrown by Leontius, one of his generals. The victorious rebel ordered the emperor's nose cut off and banished him to Kherson in the Crimea. The court camarilla figured that a noseless man was not likely to nurture any new ambitions. But they were mistaken. Justinian improved his features with a shining proboscis of solid gold and at the head of 15,000 horsemen pounced upon Constantinople—the capital. He regained his crown in 704 and ruled for another seven years. A new rebellion overthrew him in 711. This time the rebel leader made sure of his victim and killed him most effectively by cutting off his head.

HOW LONG IS
A LIGHT YEAR
?
6,000,000,000,000
MILES

THE FLUTE OF SHAME
IN OLD EUROPE MEDIOCRE *MUSICIANS* WERE PUBLICLY
PILLORIED FOR 90 DAYS WITH AN IRON FLUTE
FASTENED AROUND THEIR NECKS AND THEIR FINGERS
LOCKED TO THE FINGER HOLES
DURING THAT TIME THEY WERE THE BUTT OF PUBLIC MOCKERY

THE WORD "SOLDIER" IS DERIVED FROM THIS
ANCIENT ROMAN COIN *"SOLIDUS"*
WHICH REPRESENTED A MONTH'S PAY
FOR A ROMAN G.I.

CIRCULAR
CONDUIT
AT .82 DEPTH-
CARRIES AS MUCH WATER
AS WHEN FULL
82%
FULL

Palindromes

NO, IT IS OPPOSITION

*   *   *

SAIPPUAKAUPPIAS
(A "soapmaker" in Finnish)

*   *   *

IN GIRUM IMUS NOCTE ET CONSUMIMUR IGNI
(We gather around at night and are consumed in the fire.)
Satan's Latin answer to St. Anthony, who inquired as to how
he spends his time in the underworld.

73

ISHAM HARRIS

The Noblest Work of God

GOVERNOR ISHAM GREEN HARRIS (1818–1897) of Tennessee was a man of such towering probity that he could serve as an illustration of Alexander Pope's line: "An honest man is the noblest work of God." Governor Harris was chief executive of his state in 1861. He declared for the Confederacy and was promptly forced out of office by the Union armies. He enlisted as a private and took part in hundreds of skirmishes and battles for four years. After the surrender he went to Mexico and England—but presently returned to his native state. During the six years of marching and camping, warfare and exile he carried on his person the sum of $650,000 in cash—representing the liquid assets of the Tennessee State Public School Fund for which he had been responsible. This sum he guarded with his life through war and banishment. Although he was often in want and privation, he never touched a penny of this sacred trust. When his exile was over, he took care to surrender to the Administration of his state the original sum of $650,000 undiminished by a single cent—an act of monumental integrity that leaves the ordinary citizen speechless and humble with admiration.

A Fan Letter Made Her First Lady of the Globe

IULIA DOMNA, the daughter of an obscure priest of Baal in faraway Syria, became a Roman empress as the result of one mash note. The eighteen-year-old girl was both plain and poor. She was a provincial in a backward part of the empire. But again the power of a woman must never be under-estimated. In 186 Iulia sat down and wrote a curiously girlish epistle to the Roman Governor of Lugdunum (Lyons) in France. The little schemer told the forty-one-year-old Roman—who had recently become a widower—that she had heard of his bereavement. "I consulted an astrologer," she remarked brightly, "and had a horoscope prepared which shows that I am destined to become a queen. Marry me," she added, "and you will share my fate and be king some day." This naïve logic appealed to the superstitious Roman whose name was Septimius Severus. He made Iulia his wife the following year. Six years later Septimius became Emperor of Rome and Iulia became in fact his empress. Her son Caracalla succeeded his father on the Roman throne and two of her nephews—Alexander Severus and Elagabalus—succeeded to the imperial purple. Superstition and naïveté were the two rungs on which Iulia climbed to the dizzying heights of a throne.

IULIA DOMNA

THE BIDDENDEN MAIDS' CAKE

The Oldest "Siamese" Twins

MARY AND ALIZA CHULKHURST (1066–1100) of Biddenden, England, were joined together at the shoulders and hips and lived to the age of thirty-four. They have achieved a curious kind of immortality. By a will dated in 1100 they left their property—consisting of 20 acres of land—to the church-wardens of the parish, directing that the annual revenue be spent on cakes bearing an imprint of their effigy. The cakes were to be distributed to all strangers sojourning in Biddenden on Easter morning. In spite of the long passage of time the bequest is still in effect. If you should happen to dwell in Biddenden on a paschal morn, you will be the recipient of Biddenden cakes, a tenacious survival which bids fair to last forever.

*   *   *

ON THE SAME day that the United States went off the gold standard (1933), a reader reported that his goldfish turned to silver. This seemed like an incredible act of piscatorial patriotism, but it is made plausible by the fact that goldfish kept in a dark room will often turn white.

*   *   *

How much does your name weigh? (See answer on page 150.)

76

MILLENNIAL
MILLINERY

THE HATS worn by Greek women inhabiting a corner of the
Greek-Bulgarian border were fashioned by Alexander the
Great nearly twenty-three centuries ago and are still in style.
One soldier in Alexander's army was convicted of cowardice.
The great Macedonian conqueror singled out the entire regi-
mental unit for punishment. He ordered the regiment to remove their helmets and to bestow the martial headgear upon
their women camp followers. The king's orders were that the
women were to don the helmets as a symbol that their
bravery was superior to that of the men attainted. The curious
order of the Great Macedonian is still in effect. Today the
women descendants of the ancient camp followers still wear
cloth helmets of the same shape and size as the soldiers in
Alexander's army. The survival is undoubtedly due to their
pride in thus being singled out by the greatest conqueror the
world has ever known.

THE ONE-EYED ARMY

ARMY LIFE was so hard and cruel in 1840 that many Egyptian draftees would blind themselves in one eye to escape service. Mohammed Ali, ruler of Egypt, thereupon created two infantry regiments consisting solely of one-eyed soldiers. The two units were kept up for over fifty years.

*　　　*　　　*

ALPHONSE DE ROTHSCHILD (1827–1905), head of the famous Paris banking house, was so shocked at the indemnity imposed by Germany upon France after the War of 1870 that his hair—perfectly black at the age of forty-three—grew white in one afternoon. The indemnity was one billion dollars, paid by France in three years.

78

*　　　*　　　*

Short and Long

THE SHORT Ceylonese term "Assanka" means a number containing one, followed by 63 zeros—a vigintillion.

*　　　*　　　*

THE SERGEANT FISH is so called because it is big, bony, tough, voracious, big-mouthed and has stripes down its side like a marine.

*　　　*　　　*

A COW'S MOO was a unit of distance in India for 2,000 years. It represented the limit to which the sound would carry.

79

MR. PENNY FOUND A WALLET LOST BY MR. NICHOLS of Wilmington, Mass.

A CHURCHYARD in Swaffham Prior, England CONTAINS 2 CHURCHES ONE WITH NO STEEPLE AND THE OTHER WITH NO PEOPLE!

THE BELLS OF THE ABANDONED CHURCH SUMMON PARISHIONERS TO SERVICES IN THE NEW BUILDING

THE STRICTEST VEGETARIANS IN THE WORLD!

MEMBERS OF THE SAIVAL TRIBE India ARE FORBIDDEN TO MARRY ANYONE WHO CANNOT PROVE THAT HIS FAMILY HAS EATEN NO MEAT FOR 203 GENERATIONS —MORE THAN 4,000 YEARS!

SIR GILBERT SCOTT (1811-1878) celebrated British architect

BUILT
38 CATHEDRALS AND ABBEYS
474 CHURCHES
23 PARSONAGES
26 SCHOOLS
16 COLLEGES
58 MONUMENTS
AND 27 PUBLIC BUILDINGS!

HUANG ERH-NAN —NOTED CHINESE ARTIST

The Tongue Painter

HUANG ERH-NAN of Peiping paints with his tongue. Using his mouth as a tube and his tongue as a brush, Huang bends low over a table covered with a piece of silk and on this silken background produces the lotus flowers and butterflies of the typical Chinese masterpiece. While savoring a mouthful of thick, black Chinese ink with incongruous relish, he is able to regulate the flow smoothly and evenly. Huang enjoys his work as if sipping the black, viscous fluid were the most natural thing in the world.

*   *   *

MRS. A. A. VIAL of Greytown, Natal, South Africa, baked 150 cakes for the troops in Europe in 1941. After the cakes were baked, she missed her wedding ring and concluded that it must have slipped into one of the pastries. To avoid opening 150 cakes she sent them off to the army in Europe—with a note in each adverting to the ring. The finder was—of all people— her own son, Sergeant Ronnie Vial, who by an extraordinary coincidence was handed one of the cakes in London and found his mother's ring in it.

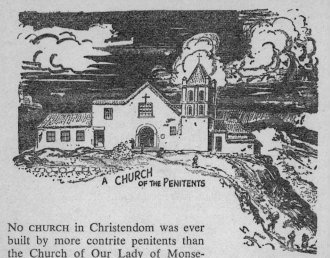

A CHURCH OF THE PENITENTS

No CHURCH in Christendom was ever built by more contrite penitents than the Church of Our Lady of Monserrate in Bogotá, Columbia. The sanctuary was built in 1626 on a mountain top towering 10,400 feet above sea level. All the bricks that went into the structure were carried to the lofty site on the backs of penitent sinners—who contributed two bricks for every transgression they felt guilty of. The severe physical ordeal of climbing to the top heavily laden must have given the repentant sinners the satisfaction of atonement. The church was built without awaiting the official permission of the king of Spain. When the monarch learned of the construction, he ordered the church torn down. His order was respectfully ignored.

*　　　*　　　*

CHARLES CARROLL of Carrollton, Md. (1737–1832), is the only signer of the Declaration of Independence who lived long enough to see a railroad. In 1828, aged ninety-one, he laid the cornerstone of the Baltimore and Ohio—the first American railway.

*　　　*　　　*

CHINESE playing cards are called "fighting sticks."

JAHANGIR (1569–1627), Mogul Emperor of India, owned the largest collection of gems in all history. His fabulous hoard included

   279,450 carats of diamonds
  2,235,600 carats of pearls
   372,600 carats of rubies
   931,500 carats of emeralds
   186,300 carats of jade

A total of 4,005,450 carats worth at least 200 million dollars.

The inventory of Jahangir's treasury was calculated not in carats but in maunds—each of which equaled 186,300 carats. He ruled India for twenty-two years—was one of

the most tolerant men, a great lover of good brandy and a great fisherman. He never kept a fish he caught, but threw it back into the water after stringing a pearl necklace through its gills. He could well afford it. His true name was Salim, but he assumed the grandiloquent name of Jahangir (Conqueror of the World) along with such titles as King of Increasing Fortune, World Gripper, Possessor of the Planets, Lord of Happenings, Index to the Book of Life and Perfect Mirror of the Glory of God.

QUEEN RANAVALONA OF MADAGASCAR
FORBADE HER SUBJECTS - UNDER PAIN OF DEATH -
TO APPEAR IN HER DREAMS - ALL WHO DID SO WERE EXECUTED

Accidents

(Selected from the "Believe It Or Not" collection of Near-Miracles)

ROBERT MERRILL of Crane, Missouri, was out hunting on October 16, 1931, when he tripped and fell. The rifle in his hand exploded and a .22-caliber bullet tore through his side. The bullet performed a neat appendectomy—shearing off Mr. Merrill's appendix "as clean as a whistle."

*   *   *

JOE FLEISHMAN of Jackson, Michigan, was smoking a pipe while fixing a tire. The tube exploded in his face, driving the pipestem deep into his throat. The stem performed a perfect tonsillectomy, severing the victim's diseased tonsils with surgical precision.

*   *   *

DURING WORLD WAR II a British submarine lay disabled on the ocean floor. After two days of frantic efforts the British Admiralty gave up all hopes of raising her. On orders of the captain the crew began to sing "Abide with Me." Sedatives were distributed to all hands. One seaman swooned and fell against some equipment. The impact set in motion the jammed surfacing apparatus. The boat rose to the surface and made port safely.

GEORGE BOTHWELL of Clintonville, Wisconsin, sold his car and two months later, as it was being towed away, it broke loose, careened down the street and crashed into his grocery store.

*   *   *

LARRY LINGLE, aged seventeen months, of Harrisburg, Pennsylvania, swallowed a nickel and coughed up a penny.

*   *   *

A ROBBER known as "the Tobin Hill bandit" unknowingly stuck up his own wife. He demanded her purse at the point of a gun and received the purse right in the face. San Antonio, Texas.

*   *   *

IN NOVEMBER 1944 a sailor on leave named Robert Dwyer entered a Service Club in Washington at 2 A.M. just in time to take part in a Bible Reading Contest. He won first prize —a long-distance phone call to his family in Louisiana. The call elicited no answer. The operator persisted in ringing and by doing so saved the family from asphyxiation by deadly gas escaping from a defective heater.

*   *   *

AN AUTOMOBILE driven by W. Schultz of Nortonville, Kansas, leaped 82 feet in the air and entered a second-story apartment through the window.

Olivette
Vernon

FRENCH WAR WIDOW
WHOSE HUSBAND
WAS KILLED IN ALGERIA
WORE
HIS SWORD AND KNAPSACK
EVERY DAY FOR 38 YEARS!

*   *   *

SERGEANT MYRON KOZIAR of San Diego, California, was shot in the throat in the Solomon Islands. The Japanese bullet merely severed his infected tonsils, leaving him otherwise unharmed and much relieved.

*   *   *

A SPEEDBOAT driven by Charles Boyd of Youngstown, Ohio, skidded 16 feet over dry land and collided with an automo-

*   *   *

THE CITY
BUILT ENTIRELY
OF SALT!

TEGAZZA in the French Sahara
MANUFACTURES SO MUCH SALT
THAT IT IS USED AS
BUILDING BLOCKS!

The Original "Bock Beer" Sign

BABYLONIAN SEAL of King Hammurabi (2200 B.C.) a contemporary of Abraham. The king and his friends are quaffing beer through golden "straws."

* * *

TAKE A BUSHEL of corn cobs—remove the kernels and the grains alone will fill the bushel.

* * *

WHAT becomes two years old the day after it is born? (See answer on page 150.)

* * *

EVERY letter is used twice in the following words:

Unensurers   Caueasus
Horseshoer   Regarage

* * *

THE BAYA BIRD of the Philippines (*Ploccus philippinus*) illuminates its nest by weaving fireflies in the web of the bower. The flies sparkle brilliantly after dark.

THE PHILIPPINE FLAG IS

REVERSED DURING WAR

*　　　　*　　　　*

WHAT HAS more legs than a centipede? (See answer on page 150.)

*　　　　*　　　　*

A BUSHEL of Pears Will Weigh
36 pounds in South Carolina
45 pounds in Nebraska
50 pounds in Pennsylvania
52 pounds in Connecticut
55 pounds in Florida
56 pounds in North Carolina
58 pounds in Vermont

*　　　　*　　　　*

THE NAME of Torquato Tasso, Italy's immortal poet, means "Chained badger."

*　　　　*　　　　*

WHICH IS THE thirty-ninth State of the Union (See answer on page 150.)

*　　　　*　　　　*

THIS MARK IS BRANDED ON THE STOMACHS OF ALL CHAMAR CHILDREN – IN INDIA – TO PREVENT COLIC.

ZENO OF ELEA, Greek philosopher ordered to reveal the names of his accomplices in a conspiracy against the tyrant of Elea, bit off his own tongue and threw it in the tyrant's face, 490 B.C.

* * *

40 DEGREES is the only point at which the Centigrade and Fahrenheit thermometers coincide exactly.

* * *

THE HEAD and the foot of an arrow are at the same end.

* * *

MARIE-ANTOINETTE did not say "Let them eat cake." What she said was "Qu'ils mangent des brioches" (Let them eat rolls). Brioche is the traditional French breakfast roll.

* * *

AMONG THE Bhuyias of India whenever a child plays hookey from school one of his parents must attend classes to make up for lost time.

* * *

BONAGUIL CASTLE, France, which was built in 1180 and has walls 11 feet thick, was literally sold for peanuts. In 1800 a grocer named Jean-Antoine Lagrave became the owner of the castle in exchange for 41 bags of peanuts.

* * *

A THIEF got away with 67 manhole covers in Little Rock, Arkansas, in 1951.

* * *

ONLY 3/10,000,000,000ths of the sun's energy reaches the earth. The loss of another 5% would destroy all human life.

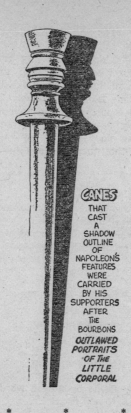

CANES THAT CAST A SHADOW OUTLINE OF NAPOLEON'S FEATURES WERE CARRIED BY HIS SUPPORTERS AFTER THE BOURBONS OUTLAWED PORTRAITS OF THE LITTLE CORPORAL

*   *   *

"THE CLOCK has stricken three," spoken by Cassius in Shakespeare's *Julius Caesar* is a striking anachronism. Striking clocks were not invented until a thousand years after Caesar.

*   *   *

"FEMININ" is masculine in French.

*   *   *

AMONG THE Nam Lo Li of Hainan, China, when a woman is found guilty of adultery her husband goes to jail.

The Beloved Bottle

THE TOMBSTONE of King Pomaré V of Tahiti is surmounted by a stone replica of a bottle of French cordial. It is there at the King's last request. Pomaré, who was the last king of Tahiti before the Society Islands were ceded to France (1880), had a monumental fondness for this well-known liqueur. Before he died in 1891, he requested the French Government to have his last resting place ornamented with a likeness of his beloved bottle so that the two may be inseparable in all eternity.

*　　　*　　　*

Epitaph of Peter Wilson
>Peter was in the ocean drowned
>A careless helpless creature
>And when his lifeless trunk was found
>It had become salt Peter
>>—Hasbro' Churchyard, England

*　　　*　　　*

ABRAHAM YSLIP of London (1821-1888) named his six sons
>Inthe Yslip
>Second Yslip
>Century Yslip
>Ofthe Yslip
>Roman Yslip
>Empire Yslip

in commemoration of the opening 8 words of Gibbon's *Decline and Fall of the Roman Empire.*

*　　　*　　　*

JUGS ARE USED AS HEADSTONES OF POTTERS IN SUGTOWN, N C

TOMBSTONE OF SAMUEL FOUGHT AND HIS WIFE Ligonier, Indiana

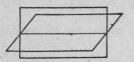

OPTICAL ILLUSION
Drawn by
BOB NUCKELS
Iron Gate, Va.

THE **GOOD NEIGHBOR TREES**
— **PIPAL TREES**
in India
ARE PLANTED INSIDE THE HOUSES AND TRAINED
TO GROW OUT THROUGH THE WINDOWS!
*THE SOUND MADE BY THE WIND AS IT RUSTLES THE BRANCHES
IS CONSIDERED MUSIC WHICH SHOULD BE SHARED WITH FRIENDS*

'A
**CORDIAL
BOTTLE**
IS CARVED
ON THE
TOMB OF
KING
POMARE V
Tahiti

*IT WAS
HIS LAST
REQUEST*

HAM AND EGGS!
HOG
THAT ADOPTED
A PULLET
Submitted by
MRS. DAN DREYER
Huntington, Ind.

COSMIC RAYS
BEFORE REACHING THE EARTH
WANDER IN INTERSTELLAR SPACE
FOR **10,000** YEARS!

WHAT IS known as Boston Cream Pie in Washington is called Washington Cream Pie in Boston.

*   *   *

LITHIUM, the lightest metal known, weighs only half as much as water.

*   *   *

A BRAND of tea known as Lung So is eaten in China as a salad.

*   *   *

A SINGLE water lily growing in a pond, doubling in size daily, will cover half of the pond in 11 days. How much of the pond will be covered in 12 days? (See answer on page 150.)

*   *   *

BLOOD is six times as thick as water.

*   *   *

WORDS beginning with *str* meaning "something extending longitudinally":

strad	streamer	strapwork	string
straddle	streel	strapworm	stringer
stradometric	street	strath	strip
straggle	stretch	stratum	stripe
straight	striae	stratus	strop
strait	striate	stray	strophe
strake	striature	streak	strunt
strand	strap	strid	struntain
stream			strut

*   *   *

THE SPEED of thought is only 150 miles an hour.

*   *   *

ALL CUNA WOMEN of San Blas, Panama, bear the name of Tutu (Flower) till the age of 12½. As soon as they are a day older, they receive an individual given name.

How MUCH does one ton of iron weigh after it has been completely rusted? (See answer on page 150.)

*   *   *

I.M.A. SAILOR was a sailor in the U. S. Navy.

*   *   *

MRS. ANN TEAK of Webster Groves, Missouri, collects antiques.

*   *   *

THE WORD "run" has 832 meanings.

*   *   *

EBONY, which is often used as a synonym of "black," can also be green, white, red, yellow, or blue. The Jamaica variety of this wood is GREEN, in the Mascarene Isles it is WHITE, on Mauritius it is RED, in the Antilles it is YELLOW, and a South American variation is BLUE.

*   *   *

THE ONLY English law that has never been broken is a statute passed by King Henry IV "prohibiting the king's subjects from transmuting base metals into gold." (5, Henry IV, c. 4.)

*   *   *

YOUR BITE requires five muscles. These muscles are the
  B uccinator
  I nternal Pterygoid
  T emporal
  E xternal Pterygoid
  M asseter

*   *   *

SPANISH MOSS is not moss at all, but a member of the pineapple family.

*   *   *

100204180 is a sentence. It reads: I ought nought to owe for I ate nothing.

One Toothache Cost 25,000 Lives

THIS EGREGIOUS toothache afflicted Queen Namasole, mother of King Mtesa of Uganda, Africa. The Queen consulted some tribal witches, who suggested to her that her ache would cease if she put the entire population of the province of Vuma to death. We don't know what the tribal witches had against the Vumians. But it is a sad fact that 25,000 men, women and children were driven into Lake Victoria where they all perished by drowning. It is also a fact that this violent remedy did not cure the Queen's toothache. History is silent about any other heroic "cures" the Queen may have attempted.

LAVOISIER

The Highest Award and the Supreme Penalty

THE MOST REGRETTED victim of the French Revolution was Antoine-Laurent Lavoisier (1743-1794), founder of Modern Chemistry and one of the great geniuses of all time. He was arrested on a trumped-up charge and sentenced to the guillotine. On the evening of May 7, 1794, a deputation consisting of four members of the French Lycée des Arts, the country's great Institute of Learning, called upon Lavoisier in his cell at the Conciergerie Prison to present him with the highest scientific award, The Wreath of Everlasting Flowers. The next day Lavoisier was executed by the guillotine. The delegates knew that their illustrious confrère was doomed—yet they risked their lives to express their sympathy with, and their admiration for, a condemned victim of the Terror.

BETWEEN 1870 and 1891 the Afghanistan postal system required its postmasters to cancel postage by biting off a piece of the stamp.

*   *   *

SAM DAVIS, a brickmaker of Greensburg, Indiana, carved his name on a brick. Thirty-one years later he moved into a house and found that the brick with his name on it was in the wall of his new home.

*   *   *

THE ISLAND OF CYCLOPS near Catania, Sicily
THIS ISLE–SHAPED LIKE A ONE-EYED GIANT–
INSPIRED HOMER'S STORY OF
ULYSSES' ENCOUNTER WITH THE CYCLOPS

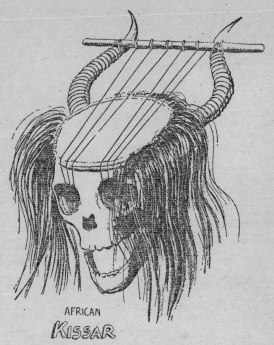

AFRICAN
KISSAR

MUSICAL INSTRUMENT MADE FROM
A HUMAN SKULL AND THE HORNS
OF A GAZELLE

*　　　　*　　　　*

'WHAT CITY in the U.S. is half golden and half silver?
(See answer on page 150.)

*　　　　*　　　　*

THE LIVER of a cod, a deep-sea fish, contains vitamins absorbed from the sun—although the cod never sees the sun.

*　　　　*　　　　*

AB. C. DEFGHI of Villa Park, Illinois, has a name in alphabetical order.

99

THE PALACE OF THE FATAL PROPHECY!

A Palace Prophecy

THE MAGNIFICENT Palace of the Tuileries in Paris was built by Queen Catherine de Médici between the years 1564 and 1566. Although she originally intended the palace as a residence for herself, she never lived in it and never even went near it. While the palace was still under construction, an astrologer told her that her death would occur in the vicinity of Saint Germain, and Saint Germain was the name of the parish within which the royal edifice was situated. Catherine kept away from the fateful parish for 23 years until she died in Blois, 200 miles away. She was given extreme unction by the Bishop of Clamecy. The name of this church dignitary was Jean de *Saint Germain* and thus the astrologer's prediction was literally fulfilled.

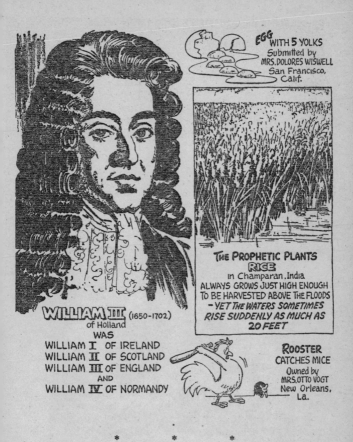

EGG WITH 5 YOLKS
Submitted by
MRS. DOLORES WISWELL
San Francisco,
Calif.

THE PROPHETIC PLANTS
RICE
In Champaran, India
ALWAYS GROWS JUST HIGH ENOUGH
TO BE HARVESTED ABOVE THE FLOODS
— YET THE WATERS SOMETIMES
RISE SUDDENLY AS MUCH AS
20 FEET

WILLIAM III (1650-1702)
of Holland
WAS
WILLIAM I OF IRELAND
WILLIAM II OF SCOTLAND
WILLIAM III OF ENGLAND
AND
WILLIAM IV OF NORMANDY

ROOSTER
CATCHES MICE
Owned by
MRS. OTTO VOGT
New Orleans,
La.

* * *

In Kenya, Africa, as soon as a woman of the Lumbwa tribe gets married her husband puts her to work growing maize. Every thirty bags of corn she produces will buy a new wife for her husband.

* * *

A 6-inch cube has the same number of square inches of surface as it has cubic inches of volume—216.

ALL THESE names of GOD have *three* letters: *

Gud	Scandinavian	Deu	Catalan
Dia	Irish	Dui	Cornish
Dio	Italian	Teo	Mexican
Bog	Russian	Kot	Ponapean
Bóg	Polish	Tyr	Icelandic
Buh	Czech	Duw	Welsh
Boh	Slovakian	Zio	High German
God	English-Netherlandish	Tiv	Gothic
Fuh	Buddhist	Tao	Chinese
SDJ	Israelite	Anu	Mesopotamian
	Sin	Babylonian	

* These are notable exceptions to the usual tetragrammatic form of the Divine Name. Beginning with the Hebrew JHVH all the other names of God consist of *four* letters.

* * *

2 ARTILLERY SHELLS
ONE AMERICAN AND THE OTHER JAPANESE
*FUSED TOGETHER BY A
HEAD-ON IMPACT IN FLIGHT!*
Battle of Mokmer Airdrome
Biak Island, N.E.I.
World War II

THE "BRAINIEST" AMERICAN WHO EVER LIVED!
Edward Henry Knight
FAMOUS PATENT LAWYER — Bellefontaine, Ohio
HAD A BRAIN WEIGHING 64 OUNCES
Daniel Webster's Brain Weighed 53½ ounces

HAROLD PARKHURST
SHAVED HIMSELF AND LIT A CIGARETTE WHILE FALLING UPSIDEDOWN IN MIDAIR — FROM AN ALTITUDE OF 20,000 FEET!
HE FELL 15,000 FEET BEFORE OPENING HIS 'CHUTE

*　　*　　*

THE ODDEST signature in the world is that of Sultan Said Ali of the Comoro Islands, a volcanic archipelago in the Indian Ocean. The signature implies a pledge to exterminate all vermin in the sultan's dominions.

*　　*　　*

AN OWL is the only bird that can look at an object with both eyes at once.

THE TENNESSEE RIVER is the only river in the United States that flows twice across a state.

*   *   *

IF THE NUMBER of children in a crowd is 43⅞ per cent of the crowd, what is the smallest number of people that could be in that crowd? (See answer on page 150.)

*   *   *

THESE twelve English words in spite of their differing spelling are pronounced alike.

are	heir
air	ayer
ayr	eyr
e'er	eir
ere	ear
eyre	ayre

*   *   *

THIRTY-FIVE pounds of air pumped into a tire increases its weight only by 3/10 pound.

*   *   *

A CUBIC INCH OF COCONUT SHELL CARBON -THE ADSORPTIVE MATERIAL USED IN GAS MASKS — CONTAINS ENOUGH SUB-MICROSCOPIC CANALS TO MAKE A TOTAL SURFACE AREA EQUAL TO 5 ACRES

RICE in India GROWS IN 80 VARIETIES

"OLD MAN MUD"
THE BIG FISH RIVER
South Africa
IS 1000 TIMES AS MUDDY
AS THE MISSISSIPPI

THE BIG WINDFALL!
A GUST OF WIND BLEW A $10 BILL
INTO FRANK VANDERHOOF'S LAP
JUST WHEN HE NEEDED EXACTLY
THAT AMOUNT FOR AN EMPLOYMENT
AGENCY FEE   New York City

PRESIDENT
JAMES MONROE
WHO DIED IN 1831
STILL RECEIVES MAIL AT HIS OLD
LAW OFFICE IN FREDERICKSBURG, VA.!

*   *   *

THERE is no wool on a mountain sheep.

*   *   *

KILTS are not of Scottish origin. They were first brought into
Scotland by a French tailor in 1745.

The Spouting Tree

A LIVE TREE from which water has been spouting for more than two generations stands in the village of Gunten on Lake Thun, Switzerland. The villagers have watered their cattle in the trough fed by the Flowing Tree for so long that they have forgotten where the water comes from. When a pipeline was first brought to the village some 60 years ago, one of the pipes was fastened to a green wooden post. Unexpectedly the post threw out roots and grew into a tree. In the process of growing, the pipe became completely embedded in the trunk and now continues to flow as if the tree contained an inexhaustible reservoir of water.

"Tarry Not at the Wine Glass"

A MOUSE
CLIMBED UP
A WINE GLASS
AND IT FELL OVER AND
TRAPPED HIM !

(BELLE WOOD,
Sacramento, Calif.)

*   *   *

THE PIKA, a rabbit found in the Canadian Rockies, is a ventriloquist. It can "throw" its shrill whistle to confuse a preying eagle.

*   *   *

NESTOR OF LARANDA, Asia Minor, rewrote *The Iliad* into twenty-four books and in each volume omitted a successive letter of the alphabet.

*   *   *

IF YOU were blindfolded and had in a drawer

26 black socks
26 white socks

How many socks would you have to take out before you could be sure that the next pair would match in color? (See answer on page 150.)

*   *   *

SHAKESPEARE mentioned America but once in all his writings. *Comedy of Errors*, Act III, Scene 2.

*   *   *

THE NOZON RIVER in Switzerland flows in two directions. It divides at the town of Pompaples. One half of the river continues south to the Mediterranean. The other half reverses its course and flows north to the North Sea.

ORIGINAL
FOUNTAIN OF LOVE

LOCATED ON GROUNDS OF OVID'S VILLA, Sulmona, Italy

THE POET OVID BELIEVED THE WATERS CONTAINED A LOVE POTION
WHICH MADE ALL WOMEN WHO DRANK OF IT FALL IN LOVE WITH HIM

*　　　*　　　*

How MANY books in the Bible? Count the letters in:
Old—3   Testament—9
$$(3 \text{ and } 9 = 39)$$
New—3   Testament—9
$$(3 \times 9 = 27)$$
Total number of books in the
　Bible   66

THE STRANGE SCARECROW STOREHOUSES OF THE SUDAN
Africa

RICE GRANARIES ARE BUILT IN THE SHAPE OF GROTESQUE MASKS IN THE BELIEF THAT RODENTS WILL BE FRIGHTENED TO DEATH!

* * *

SOUND will travel through granite 11 times as fast as through the air.

* * *

THE SCORPION will sting itself to death if touched with a drop of whisky.

The First Side-Saddle

THE FIRST equestrienne to ride side-saddle was Anne of Bohemia (1366–1394), daughter of the German Emperor Charles IV and Queen of Richard II of England. She was afflicted with a deformity which precluded her from straddling a horse. Besides, one of her legs was shorter than the other. She made a virtue out of a necessity and introduced the side-saddle to the world of fashion. The innovation was accepted because her affliction remained a secret.

PRONOUNCE them!

Krs	Brs
Crn	Strbr
Srdj	Vrb
Grn	Krn
Trstj	

Names of towns in Yugoslavia

*   *   *

A NEWSPAPER made of rubber to be read while bathing was published for several years in Paris by Aurélien Scholl.

*   *   *

CORN means oats in Scotland and Ireland—and wheat in England.

*   *   *

ONLY NINETY years ago a word was still a high-priced commodity. In 1867 Ismail I, Viceroy of Egypt, paid $300,000 for a one-word title. The money was paid to Fuad Pasha, Grand Vizier of Turkey, as a bribe to induce the Sultan of Turkey to bestow one word, "Khedive," as a title upon Ismail. Egypt was at that time a nominal vassal of the Turkish monarch.

The TOMB OF A PARTICLE

Luiz Vaz de Camões 1524-1580 PORTUGAL'S GREATEST POET
DIED IN POVERTY AND IT IS *NOT KNOWN WHERE HIS BODY IS BURIED* — AND SO
DUST WAS *GATHERED FROM ALL THE PLACES WHERE CAMÕES VISITED IN HIS LIFE*
AND *BURIED IN AN ORNATE TOMB* —

— *WITH THE HOPE THAT THIS DUST MIGHT*
CONTAIN A PARTICLE OF CAMÕES' BODY

The MEANDER RIVER

THE CROOKED RIVER PROVERBIAL FOR ITS MANY WINDINGS —
AND FROM WHICH WE OBTAINED THE WORD "MEANDER"

Asia Minor to the Aegean Sea

ARISTOPHON (412–354 B.C.), Athenian legislator, was impeached 75 times and never once convicted.

* * *

GOLDFISH with a hawthorn shrub growing from its head. Reported in Fortuna, California.

* * *

ATTA ATTA resides in Ata, province of Attica, Greece.

* * *

THE AMPERSAND (&) was formerly the twenty-seventh letter of the alphabet.

* * *

SODIUMditolyldiazobetanaphthylaminesirsulphonicbetanaphthylaminethreesixdisulphonate—a word containing eighty-four letters—refers to a Congo Red Dye.

* * *

ANDRE PUIOM of Riom, France, committed suicide for the silliest of all reasons. He discovered that his name was an anagram of *Pendu à Riom* (hanged at Riom). So he hanged himself in 1732.

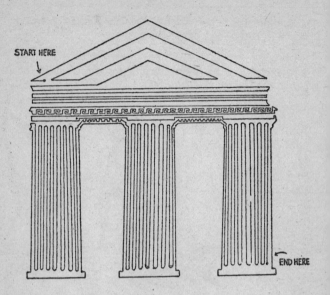

START HERE

END HERE

DRAWN IN A SINGLE LINE

*　　　*　　　*

SNOWBALLS saved a church from destruction. When the Beth-Shiloh Presbyterian Church of York, S.C., caught fire, it was extinguished with snowballs hurled by the congregation.

*　　　*　　　*

THE OLDEST known cattle brand used by the chiefs of the Bakhtiari nomads of Iran 2,000 years ago. After being used as a cattle brand, it was made the emblem of the Great Seal of Iran for several centuries.

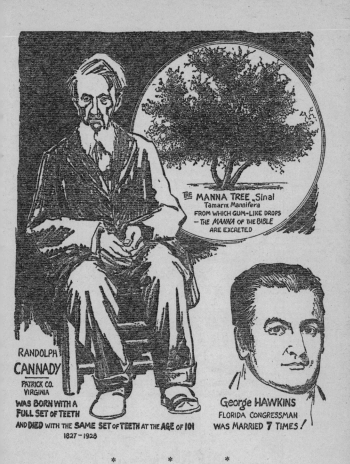

RANDOLPH **CANNADY**
PATRICK CO.
VIRGINIA
WAS BORN WITH A
FULL SET OF TEETH
AND **DIED** WITH THE **SAME SET** OF **TEETH** AT THE **AGE** OF **101**
1827 – 1928

THE **MANNA TREE** „Sinai
Tamarix Mannifera
FROM WHICH GUM-LIKE DROPS
– THE *MANNA* OF THE BIBLE
ARE EXCRETED

George **HAWKINS**
FLORIDA CONGRESSMAN
WAS MARRIED **7** TIMES!

* * *

THE NORMAL human eye is the same size in all individuals, approximately 24 mm.

* * *

THE NUMBER of rail-clicks you hear in twenty seconds is the number of miles per hour the train is traveling.

SECONDHAND STATUE!

A SECONDHAND STATUE OF LORD BYRON
WAS PURCHASED in London and ERECTED in Guayaquil,
Ecuador, IN HONOR OF JOSE J. OLMEDO (1780-1847),
FAMOUS POET, BECAUSE A MADE-TO-ORDER MEMORIAL
WOULD COST TOO MUCH!

The Gingerbread Tree

THE DOUM PALM of Egypt, the only palm that has branches, bears fruit that tastes like gingerbread.

*   *   *

A MACKEREL will drown in a small tank of water. If it were forced to swim slowly, the current produced by the movement of the gills would not supply enough oxygen to allow the fish to live.

*   *   *

WHAT KIND of clock shows the exact time twice a day—but is wrong at all other times? (See answer on page 150.)

*   *   *

WHAT book has its preface in the middle, its end in the beginning and its climax before the plot? (See answer on page 150.)

*   *   *

WILLIAM D. GRAHAM of Silver Springs, Florida, sat in the same chair on his golden wedding anniversary in which his father and grandfather sat on their respective golden wedding days.

*   *   *

JOHN bought 10 cents' worth of cheese. Jim bought 6 cents' worth of crackers. Joe gave the boys 16 cents as his share. How are John and Jim to divide Joe's money? (See answer on page 150.)

Optical Illusion

IF YOU gaze at it steadily it will appear to spin.

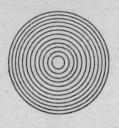

*　　　*　　　*

THE WORD "dun" is derived from the name of Joe Dun, bailiff of Lincoln, England, in the time of Henry VII. He was so successful in collecting debts that his name became a synonym for "urging payment."

*　　　*　　　*

A TOOTH of Sir Isaac Newton was purchased by Lord Shaftesbury for 730 pounds ($3,650) in 1816.

A Dog Was Made King

KING EYSTEIN Illrade of Norway made his greyhound "Saur" king of the district of Trondheim to punish its people for an uprising led by Kettil Jamte, a native of the district.

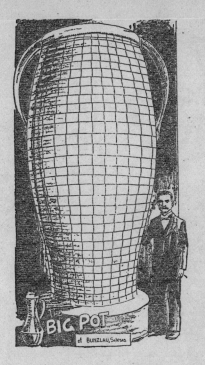

The Pot of Love

THE TOWN of Bunzlau, Silesia, Germany, which specializes in pottery, is still proud of a gigantic piece of crockery fashioned by a lovelorn potter's assistant named Joppe to gain the hand of his master's daughter. The pot, a true labor of love, was created in 1753. When he exhibited his masterpiece and the city fathers realized its capacity of 30 bushels of peas, they interceded with the obdurate father till he gave his consent. The city of Bunzlau was so enchanted with this success that they have been treasuring the Pot of Love *(Liebestopf)* ever since and even adopted it as the city emblem.

The ROCK THAT WAS A BATTLESHIP "H.M.S. DIAMOND ROCK" WAS LONG LISTED AS A BRITISH BATTLESHIP IN RECOGNITION OF THE BRAVERY OF THE CREW WHO DEFENDED IT AGAINST THE FRENCH FOR 18 MONTHS (1804-5)

WOMEN ON THE ISLAND of DOMINICA - SPEAK A DIFFERENT LANGUAGE FROM THE MEN!

—

THEIR HUSBANDS WILL _NOT_ TEACH THEM ANYTHING

FIRST TO SALUTE THE AMERICAN FLAG!
Governor Johannes de Graaff
St. Eustatius, Dutch West Indies, on Nov 16, 1776
FIRED A 21-GUN SALUTE TO THE AMERICAN FLAG
HE WAS DISMISSED FOR SUCH AN UNLAWFUL ACT!

THE MIDNIGHT MAN of WÜRTTEMBERG
BARON HERMAN MITTNACHT (Meaning: MIDNIGHT)

Midnighthood

BARON HERMAN VON MITTNACHT (1825–1909), Prime Minister of the State of Württemberg, Germany, for thirty-nine years, was so preoccupied with the significance of his surname that it is a wonder he found time for any other activity. Mittnacht is an adaptation of the German word for "midnight." The baron had the foresight to be born at midnight and he married at midnight. Throughout life he ate the main repast of the day at midnight, and insisted that all his appointments to office be signed at midnight. He named his pet dog Midnight, hired two servants named Midnight, patronized only tradesmen either named Midnight or at least born at midnight. He was the godfather of all Suabian boys who were his namesakes, 118 of them. He took his annual vacation in the Land of the Midnight Sun (Norway) and bequeathed his fortune in trust—providing that the income be paid each year to the first virtuous maiden, either named Midnight or born at midnight, who was willing to marry a man named Midnight. And he crowned his life's ambition by actually departing this life on the stroke of midnight.

JOHN WHITEAKER (1831–1902) was elected governor of the State of Oregon before there was such a state. State elections anticipated Congressional action in 1858. The newly elected chief executive had to wait till the U.S. Congress admitted the State of Oregon—before he could enter upon his duties.

* * *

THE BRITTLE Star breaks off its arms when alarmed, leaving only the central disc.

* * *

LOBSTERS in sealed cans live longer than those shipped in containers with air vents.

* * *

CAN YOU multiply two figures—each containing the 9 digits only once—and obtain a product with the 9 digits? (See answer on page 150.)

* * *

TRY THIS tongue twister:
The old scold sold a school coal scuttle.

The KIWI-KIWI
Wingless Bird
LAYS EGGS ¼ ITS OWN SIZE

I PROMISE
NEVER TO
MARRY
AGAIN
JACK

EVERGREEN CEMETERY
Jacksonville, Florida

The
OLD
LADY
of ILOK
FAMOUS
PEPPER SELLER
OF YUGO-SLAVIA
WORKED
DAILY
FOR 100 YEARS —
AT THE SAME JOB!

THE OLD GUARD DIES!

The Useless Watch

FOR 123 YEARS after Napoleon's death, the municipal authorities of Rye, England, maintained an armed sentry over the Strait of Dover to watch for the return of the Great Corsican. The watch was instituted in 1802 when Bonaparte made preparations to invade the British Isles from Boulogne. Although the Napoleonic star set definitely with the death of the Great Corsican in 1821, the guard was never abandoned. Its sharp-eyed duties were handed down from father to son till it reached Chummy Barton—the last of the line. Right through the menace of Kaiserism and Hitlerism Chummy continued to guard the country against Napoleon till he died in 1944. Only then did the patriotic city fathers disband the 142-year-old guard—together with the annual dotation of $20. The Napoleonic specter was considered banished forever.

The Water Drill

CZAR NICHOLAS I of Russia (1825–1855) compelled his recruits to practice the goosestep while bearing upon their tall headgear a glass full of water. If a soldier spilled as much as a single drop, he was obliged to serve an additional year for every drop he spilled.

Beer Barrel Tombstone
of Humphrey Wood
Kirkheaton, England

*   *   *

Here lies the body of Jonathan Blake
Stepped on the gas
Instead of the brake

       —Gravestone near Uniontown, Pa.

*   *   *

Thankfull
His wife died

       —Gravestone in Houghton, N.Y.
       (Thankfull was his wife's name.)

*   *   *

Here lies Liz
Who She is
Is nobody's biz

       —Gravestone in Orange County, Virginia

*   *   *

Bertha
Bright
Sparks
May the Bright Sparks Upward Fly

       —Epitaph in Graveyard
       Near Council Bluffs, Iowa

*   *   *

Here Lies
Lotta Dust   —Roselawn Cemetery, Detroit, Mich.

THE ARMENIANS USE LAMB-SHAPED TOMBSTONES!
THE LAMB BEING THE SYMBOL OF CHRIST

*   *   *

An Honest Man
Is the noblest work of God
    Here lies
  An honest woman
             —Bottisham Churchyard, Cambridge, England

*   *   *

Elisha Bowman
Died March 21, 1865
He believed that nothing
But the Democratic Party
Will ever save the Union
          —Mead Cemetery, Washington County, Indiana

*   *   *

Tombstone commemorating the hat, cane and chair of the
deceased.   —Naples, Ill.

A SPECIES of shrimp *(Thermosbaena mirabilis)*, found in the hot springs of the Oasis of El Hamma, Tunisia, is caught already cooked.

*   *   *

A CHOCOLATE-covered almond sprouted in a candy bar.
    Reported by Mrs. Joseph Riede, Denver, Colorado.

*   *   *

CAN YOU remove 4 letters from a 5-letter word—without altering the pronunciation? (See answer on page 150.)

*   *   *

THE WEATHER vane does not point in the direction of the wind. It points the opposite way.

*   *   *

WOOD of the Lignum Vitae Tree cannot be split owing to the diagonal and oblique arrangement of its fibers.

*   *   *

THE CHINESE ideographs for time of day are taken from pupil contraction in the eye of a cat.

(I) NOON   (O) 6 P.M.   (O) MIDNIGHT

THE CHINESE ideograph for "slander" contains three symbols
—WORDS MOUNTAIN MOUTH—meaning "Making a
mountain out of a molehill."

*　　　　*　　　　*

THE WORD AYE rearranged still has the same meaning—YEA.

*　　　　*　　　　*

THE SNAKE-NECKED turtle of Australia has a neck too long
to be drawn into its shell—it is folded sideways.

*　　　　*　　　　*

THE EARTH is neither round nor flat. It is a Geoid.

*　　　　*　　　　*

THE HEART OF STONE
Fyellenbacker, Norway

THE HEART-SHAPED rock of Fyellenbacker, Norway, is suspended over a path which has long been used as a Lover's
Lane.

*　　　　*　　　　*

THE PADAUK plant of Burma performs a useful function as a
barometer. Its blossoming always presages the beginning of
the rainy season within twenty-four hours.

BLIND SCHOLAR
HANAWA HOKIICHI of Musashi, Japan

The Blind Colossus

HANAWA HOKIICHI (1722–1823), a native of the province of Musashi, Japan, was one of the most towering scholars in the history of civilization. He crowded into his busy life the activities of a legion of geniuses. He became blind at the age of seven and dedicated the remaining ninety-four years of darkness to the task of teaching and writing on a scale that was the wonder of his age. His memory was so capacious that he could store within it the contents of more than 400,000 manuscripts, collected during a lifetime. From these scrolls—none of which could have been read to him more than once—he compiled the *Gunsho Ruiju,* a work of 2,820 volumes—the most voluminous book ever published. It was republished in 1910 and has served as a priceless reference work for generations of Japanese students and historians. The BLIND GIANT also founded an institution known as the Wagakuso School, where he taught the Japanese classics, "reading" to classes for days at a time—from books he could not see. A favorite Japanese painting represents Hokiichi lecturing to an audience enveloped in darkness—oblivious of the fact that the light had gone out many hours before.

THE NATIVE banana (plantain) is never cut crosswise in the Canary Islands. A plantain so sliced reveals the outline of a cross in each section.

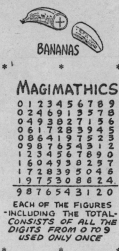

BANANAS

* * *

MAGIMATHICS

```
0 1 2 3 4 5 6 7 8 9
0 2 4 6 9 1 3 5 7 8
0 4 9 3 8 2 7 1 5 6
0 6 1 7 2 8 3 9 4 5
0 8 6 4 1 9 7 5 2 3
0 9 8 7 6 5 4 3 1 2
1 2 3 4 5 6 7 8 9 0
1 6 0 4 9 3 8 2 5 7
1 7 2 8 3 9 5 0 4 6
1 9 7 5 3 0 8 6 2 4.
```
9 8 7 6 5 4 3 1 2 0

EACH OF THE FIGURES
-INCLUDING THE TOTAL-
CONSISTS OF ALL THE
DIGITS FROM 0 TO 9
USED ONLY ONCE

* * *

THE STRANGEST MUSEUM IN THE WORLD: A COUNTERFEITERS' MUSEUM HOUSED IN THE HOLLOW TRUNK OF AN ANCIENT PINE TREE. Lillehammer, Norway.

THE MÁLEO BIRD LAYS AN EGG NEARLY AS BIG AS *ITSELF*

The Man Who Wrote After Death

A DEAD CHINESE courtier named Ling Wen hurled the epithet of "traitor" at the Chinese Emperor Yung Lo (1360-1424). The greatest of the Ming emperors had sentenced his courtier to death for insulting him to his face. While the executioner was sent for, some bystanders counseled the culprit to implore the Emperor's mercy so that he might rescind the death sentence. But Ling Wen refused, saying: "Even after I am dead, I shall continue to brand him a traitor." And it came to pass that after his head was chopped off, the blood, oozing from the severed neck into the sand, formed a perfect Chinese ideograph of the word "traitor" before the Emperor's shocked gaze. "He had the last word," he murmured. Yung Lo was so unnerved, he transferred the seat of government from Nanking to Peiping, which has been the Chinese capital ever since.

THE BULLET THAT FOUND ITS MARK AFTER 20 YRS!

IN 1893 HENRY ZIEGLAND, Honey Grove, Tex. JILTED HIS SWEETHEART WHO KILLED HERSELF. HER BROTHER TRIED TO AVENGE HER BY SHOOTING ZIEGLAND BUT THE BULLET ONLY GRAZED HIS FACE AND BURIED ITSELF IN A TREE. THE BROTHER, THINKING HE HAD KILLED ZIEGLAND, COMMITTED SUICIDE.

IN 1913, ZIEGLAND WAS CUTTING DOWN THE TREE WITH THE BULLET IN IT — IT WAS A TOUGH JOB SO HE USED DYNAMITE AND *THE EXPLOSION SENT THE OLD BULLET THRU ZIEGLAND'S HEAD–KILLING HIM*

HERE LIES THE BODY OF JANE GORDON WITH MOUTH ALMIGHTY AND TEETH ACCORDIN'.

GRAVE MARKER IN MARBLEHEAD, MASS.

OSTRICH EGG
LARGEST SINGLE CELL IN THE WORLD

*　　　*　　　*

DOCTORS have furnished forty saints to the church. Three of the Popes were originally physicians: John XXII, Paul II and Nicholas V.

*　　　*　　　*

SWEDISH history lists six kings who never existed. They were Charles I, II, III, IV, V, VI. The first real Charles was King Charles VII, who ruled from 1155 to 1167.

THE CASTLE OF THE VARIABLE ECHO!
Lucera, Italy
ITS WALLS REPEAT EVERY SOUND 11 TIMES DURING THE DAY BUT 12 TIMES AFTER SUNDOWN!

TAMERLANE
Mongol Conqueror
PLAYED A GAME OF POLO AFTER EACH VICTORIOUS BATTLE -USING AS A BALL- THE HEAD OF THE DEFEATED ENEMY GENERAL!

THE MAHOUT

Which Is the Oldest Language Still in Use?

It is the language employed by the Indian mahout—the professional elephant driver and keeper. In addressing the elephant the mahout uses neither Hindi nor Arabic nor Persian. Instead he employs the tongue of the caveman—with which the latter first tamed an elephant 50,000 years ago. This survival—one of the most astounding in history—furnishes some basis for the traditional elephant memory since the pachyderm still refuses to understand any other tongue.

Cows with Gold Teeth

SOME YEARS ago in the vicinity of the Alder Creek Gold Mines, Wenatchee, Washington, the teeth of grazing cows became permanently coated with free gold dust from their pasture in the Alder Creek basin. Several bovine jawbones with gold-filled teeth have been preserved for skeptical posterity. The lime in the teeth combined with the gold dust to form a perfect and permanent dental crown.

*   *   *

THE DISTANCE by boat from New York to Manila is
  via Panama Canal—13,289 miles
  via Suez Canal—13,288 miles

*   *   *

PRESIDENT HAYES spent
  4 years in college
  4 years in Congress
  4 years as Governor
  4 years in the Civil War
was wounded 4 times and served
  4 years as President.

*   *   *

THE LUCKY 13

THIRTEEN is considered the luckiest of all omens in Italy. Girls wear talismans featuring 13 as a protector from evil.

VIRGINIA IS FARTHER WEST THAN WEST VIRGINIA

AN **ELM TREE** WAS ELECTED A MEMBER OF THE COMMUNIST PARTY
Ural, Russia

ROGER SHERMAN IS THE *ONLY* AMERICAN WHO SIGNED THESE 4 HISTORIC DOCUMENTS
ARTICLES OF ASSOCIATION
DECLARATION OF INDEPENDENCE
ARTICLES OF CONFEDERATION
U.S. CONSTITUTION

A TEA KETTLE IS *NOT* A TEA KETTLE IT IS A WATER KETTLE

OPTICAL ILLUSION
THE SQUARES ARE PERFECT

EAGLE MOUNTAIN
Manhart, Italy
NATURAL FORMATION

137

The Only GI President

LINCOLN was the only president of the United States whose last military rank—prior to becoming the Chief Executive —was that of a simple private in the army. Private Lincoln served from May 27 to July 10, 1833, and his pay was 21 cents a day.

* * *

L. E. DITTO OF RIPLEY, Tennessee, became the father of twins at the age of seventy-one—his twenty-first and twenty-second child.

* * *

THE JAPANESE numeral 13 resembles a tombstone.

* * *

THIS WOODEN object will roll UP an incline instead of DOWN.

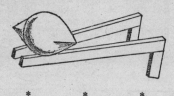

* * *

THE CANADIAN Jumping Fern travels by rooting fresh plants at the end of its fronds.

BINGO
in England
IS
CALLED
HOUSIE
HOUSEY

THE ELEPHANT IS THE ONLY ANIMAL WITH 4 KNEES

THE **MEN** WHO GO SAILING IN TUBS
Wuhu, China
BEGGARS PADDLE OUT TO MEET STEAMERS ON THE YANGTZE RIVER *IN WOODEN WASHTUBS!*

THE **STRANGEST** ARBITER OF FASHION IN HISTORY!
Modena, Italy
A **MARBLE STATUE** BUILT IN 1473 AS A LEGAL YARDSTICK OF THE MAXIMUM LENGTH AT WHICH LADIES COULD WEAR THEIR DRESSES!

THOSE WEARING LONGER TRAINS WERE PUNISHED FOR STIRRING UP DUST

THE MAN WHO CAUGHT A LEOPARD BY THE TAIL!
SANTAL RAKHAL of Raipur, India—SURPRISED A LEOPARD WITH ITS TAIL PROTRUDING THROUGH A TRELLIS — AND HUNG ON UNTIL HIS BROTHER STUNNED IT WITH A CLUB!

MULTIPLY any number of 5 digits by 11—then by 9,091 and the original number will reappear twice in the product.

* * *

THE FLOWER pots used by King Abbad el Motaddid of Seville, who died February 28, 1069, were made from the skulls of enemies the king killed with his own hands.

CAT BORN ON THE STETTER RANCH KENNEDY, Neb., WITH THEIR CATTLE BRAND ON ITS SIDE

* * *

MOSQUITOES prefer blondes but they are not gentlemen. Only female mosquitoes "bite" and they consider the skin of a blonde less resistant.

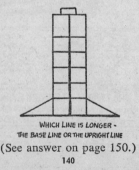

WHICH LINE IS LONGER -
THE BASE LINE OR THE UPRIGHT LINE

(See answer on page 150.)

Soul Windows

BEDROOMS in the Canton of Grisons, Switzerland, are equipped with a tiny window—to be opened when the occupant is dying so that his soul may escape.

* * *

THE TAIL of a comet is so incredibly tenuous that 60,000 cubic miles of it will weigh as much as the air you inhale in a single breath.

* * *

144740111546645244279463731260859884815736774914748-35889066354349131199152128 is the largest perfect number known—being the sum of all its divisors.

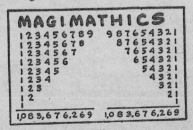

12 X 483 = 5796
4 X 1738 = 6952
4 X 1963 = 7852
42 X 138 = 5796
48 X 159 = 7632
*EACH PROBLEM CONTAINS
ALL 9 DIGITS - USED ONCE*

DICK ALLEN - Happy, Texas - BORN WITHOUT EARS or EAR OPENINGS COULD HEAR DISTINCTLY THRU HIS MOUTH AND BECAME AN EXCELLENT MUSICIAN !

THE **SWORD** OF **KING CHARLES I** of Spain HAS BEEN IMBEDDED IN THE WALLS OF PERPIGNAN , FRANCE **FOR 412 YEARS**

IN 1542 - WHILE THE TOWN WAS A SPANISH POSSESSION - THE KING FOUND A SENTRY SLEEPING ON DUTY AND 'STOOD GUARD FOR HIM UNTIL THE SOLDIER AWAKENED

THE U.S. HAS OBSERVED *ONLY ONE-NATIONAL HOLIDAY IN ITS ENTIRE HISTORY* CONGRESS SO DESIGNATED *APRIL 30,1889* - THE CENTENNIAL ANNIVERSARY OF GEORGE WASHINGTON'S INAUGURATION AS THE FIRST PRESIDENT

EACH HOUR USING FUEL ENOUGH TO TRAVEL 'ROUND THE WORLD ! FAST MODERN TURBOJETS MAY USE UP FUEL AT THE RATE OF 1000 TO 2000 GALLONS AN HOUR, OFTEN ENOUGH TO DRIVE A MOTORCAR 1½ TIMES AROUND THE WORLD AT THE EQUATOR.

142

Armand
Jacques
Lherbette

The Dreamless Lawyer

ARMAND-JACQUES L'HERBETTE of Paris (1791–1864) never slept in seventy-one years. He suffered a skull fracture when as a child of two he watched the execution of King Louis XVI on January 21, 1793. The observation stand occupied by the boy and his parents collapsed in a heap and he was taken to a hospital in an unconscious condition. After his recovery he never shut his eyes in slumber during the remaining threescore and eleven years of his life. A brain injury which caused his life-long insomnia did not prevent him from becoming a celebrated lawyer and notary. He was most widely known as "The Legal Light that is never extinguished."

143

THE NUTCRACKER ROCK

Nutcracker Rock

THE GIGANTIC pierced rock on the Island of Ebulon in the Gulf of Siam has one movable jaw and looks like a nutcracker. At low tide the two jaws gape about 10 feet. The high tide swings one jaw of the nutcracker against the other with such force that a pebble placed between them or even a nut is instantly crushed.

*   *   *

THE ATLANTIC and the Pacific Oceans have exactly the same level during one month of the year, in February. During the other eleven months of the year the level of the Pacific is higher than that of the Atlantic.

The SWORD-BILL HUMMING-BIRD HAS A BILL LONGER THAN ITS BODY

BOUNCING WATERFALL
Cascade des Pelerins, Chamonix, France
A MOST SINGULAR AND BEAUTIFUL PHENOMENON
THE TORRENT FALLS OVER A CLIFF AND, STRIKING A ROCK BASIN, IT REBOUNDS 60 FEET INTO THE AIR IN A PARABOLIC ARCH

JACOB VAN NISSEN of Zwolle, Holland, MARRIED AN 18-YEAR-OLD GIRL HIS SON MARRIED HIS STEPMOTHER'S 40-YEAR-OLD MOTHER AND THUS BECAME HIS OWN *GRANDFATHER*

OPTICAL ILLUSION
WHICH WAY IS THE ELEPHANT STANDING?

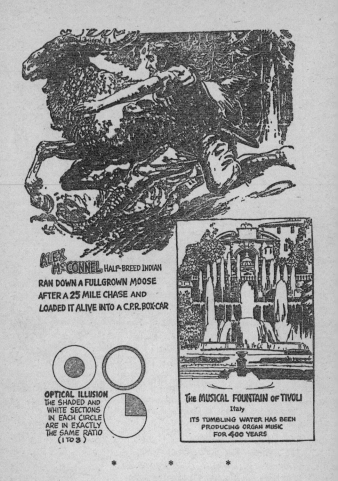

ALEX McCONNEL HALF-BREED INDIAN RAN DOWN A FULLGROWN MOOSE AFTER A 25 MILE CHASE AND LOADED IT ALIVE INTO A C.P.R. BOX-CAR

OPTICAL ILLUSION THE SHADED AND WHITE SECTIONS IN EACH CIRCLE ARE IN EXACTLY THE SAME RATIO (1 TO 3)

THE MUSICAL FOUNTAIN OF TIVOLI Italy

ITS TUMBLING WATER HAS BEEN PRODUCING ORGAN MUSIC FOR 400 YEARS

* * *

THE LETTERS *O*, *B*, *P*, and *F* are pictorial in origin. *O* is the open mouth in the act of uttering the sound. *B* shows the profile of the sealed human lips pronouncing it. *P* is the lips partly open and *F* is a *P* with the air escaping.

A CARAVAN OF 20 PEOPLE FROZE TO DEATH ON THE EQUATOR BENEATH A BRILLIANT TROPICAL AFRICAN SKY! 1908

TWENTY MEN FROZE to death on the equator beneath a brilliant tropical African sun.

In February 1908 Baron Egon von Kirchstein led a caravan of 40 men in an attempt to conquer one of the world's mightiest volcanoes, the 14,500-foot-high Mount Karissimbi of the Virunga Range in Ruanda, Central Africa. The volcano straddles the equator.

They endured incredible cold for several days before they reached the Branca Crater, 12,000 feet above sea level. Here the howling of an icy wind suddenly increased to the fury of a hurricane. It was high noon but the cold grew very intense in spite of a tropical sun blazing overhead. The obliquity of the ground added to the force of the tempest and made the erection of tents impossible. Wearing sunglasses against the blinding glare, the members of the caravan huddled close together for warmth, for what seemed like an eternity. The air grew more and more glacial until death began to still the chattering teeth of the sufferers. Around 6 o'clock in the afternoon the arctic wind abated and the survivors began a grim stocktaking. Fully half of the caravan lay dead on the icy ground still wearing their grotesque spectacles against the setting sun. Twenty men died between 12 noon and 6 p.m. on February 28, 1908, frozen to death under a blazing tropical sun.

COUNT ISTVAN SZECHENYI – FAMOUS HUNGARIAN SCIENTIST (1791–1860)
WENT INSANE AND CHESS
WAS PRESCRIBED AS A CURE
A YOUNG STUDENT WAS
HIRED TO PLAY CHESS
WITH THE OLD COUNT
– AT THE END OF 6 YRS.
THE COUNT RECOVERED
HIS REASON – AND THE
STUDENT BECAME
INCURABLY INSANE!

The
COAT OF BROBDINGNAGIAN BRIGHT
COULD HOLD 7 MEN BUTTONED
INSIDE OF IT

THE **YAK**
HAS THE HEAD OF A COW – TAIL OF A HORSE
SKELETON OF A BISON – THE HAIR OF A GOAT
HORNS OF AN OX AND THE **GRUNT OF A PIG.**

* * *

The River Sentenced to Death and Executed

THE GYNDES River—now known as the Diala—in Iraq—
is the only river in history to suffer this unique fate. The
judge in the case was no less a personality than the great
Cyrus, king of Persia. In crossing the Gyndes one day the
king lost one of his sacred white horses by drowning. In the

THE BOILING SEA
Isle of Ischia, Italy
THE WATER
IN THE HARBOR OF FORIO
IS SO HOT IT BOILS EGGS
IT IS HEATED BY SUBTERRANEAN
VOLCANIC FIRES

HERE'S MUD IN YOUR EYE
SEPTIMIA PATABINIANA
BALBILLA TYRIA!

ROMANS
DRINKING TO A LADY'S
HEALTH *QUAFFED ONE
CUP OF WINE FOR
EVERY LETTER IN
HER NAME*

The CRUEL
PHILANTHROPIST
DULU MURAD KHAN—ruler of Rawalpindi, India
GAVE EVERY BEGGAR WHO ACCOSTED HIM
EITHER A LAKH OF RUPEES ($48,500)
OR DEATH!
*THE DEATH SENTENCE WAS ADMINISTERED WHEN
DULU KHAN WAS SHORT OF FUNDS*
—BECAUSE HE COULD NOT BEAR TO SAY "NO"

eyes of the king the river forfeited its life. Capital punishment was meted out with dispatch to the stream. The king ordered 360 channels dug to divert the waters of the Gyndes. The river ceased to exist and its death lasted a thousand years. It was revived when the sands of the desert dried up the channels, resurrecting the dead water course and canceling the king's strange death sentence.

THE ANSWERS

14—Yes, the water level will drop.

14—32.

14—55.

14—BOOB-BOOKKEEPER.

20—East-West lines of latitude are parallel but North-South lines of longitude are not. Your trip, therefore, would not bring you back to your starting point.

33—A moment is an old English unit of time—equal to 1½ minutes.

37—3 feet.

39—Abraham Lincoln and Jefferson Davis.

51—2 feet.

58—The larger the brush, the greater the effort; hence he will require *twice* the time.

76—Each letter of your name written in pencil weighs .0000125 of an ounce.

88—A race horse.

89—An earthworm. It has nearly 1200 legs.

89—Nobody knows which is the 39th and which is the 40th state. North and South Dakota were admitted on the same day and President Harrison kept the text covered while signing both proclamations.

94—All of it.

95—Three tons.

99—DEN-VER   golden   silver

104—800.

107—3.

117—A stopped clock. The stopped hands will indicate the correct time for an instant twice each day.

117—The Dictionary.

117—John 12 cents—Jim 4 cents.

122—$246913578 \times 987654312 = 493827156^2$

128—Q u e u e.

140—They are both the same length.